Contraband
COCKTAILS

C.1

Contraband
COCKTAILS

HOW AMERICA DRANK WHEN
IT WASN'T SUPPOSED TO

PAUL DICKSON

MELVILLE HOUSE
BROOKLYN · LONDON

CONTRABAND COCKTAILS

Copyright © 2015 by Paul Dickson
First Melville House printing: November 2015

Grateful acknowledgment is made to the Library of Congress
for permission to reprint photographs from their archive.

Melville House Publishing		8 Blackstock Mews
46 John Street	and	Islington
Brooklyn, NY 11201		London N4 2BT

mhpbooks.com   facebook.com/mhpbooks   @melvillehouse

Library of Congress Cataloging-in-Publication Data
Dickson, Paul, author.
  Contraband cocktails : how America drank when it wasn't
supposed to / Paul Dickson.
    pages cm
    Includes bibliographical references.
    ISBN 978-1-61219-458-5 (hardback)
    ISBN 978-1-61219-459-2 (ebook)
    1. Cocktails. 2. Cocktails—United States—History. I. Title.
TX951.D499 2015
  641.87'4—dc23

                                        2015030030

Design by Adly Elewa

Printed in the United States of America
10 9 8 7 6 5 4 3 2 1

CONTENTS

PREFACE

Much has been written about Prohibition in the United States (1920–1933), but precious little has been written about the paradoxical rise of the cocktail and the stylish, urbane "cocktail culture" that began to flower on the very date—January 16, 1920—when mixed drinks and all other forms of alcohol became illegal.

This book attempts to remedy the situation with a discourse on Prohibition cocktails followed by an annotated formulary of drinks from the Dry Years, including many drinks that were created during the period by expatriate American bartenders.

Almost a hundred years after the fact, Prohibition still holds a deep fascination for Americans. At the most superficial and visible level, it survives in the many Prohibition Era faux speakeasies that dot the landscape. The speakeasy revival began in the late twentieth century with an occasional novelty, and continued to rise steadily through to the first decade of the twenty-first century, at the end of which it boomed.

Take the city of Boston. As of this writing, it had a dozen Prohibition-themed bars and restaurants, such as the Carrie Nation Restaurant and Bar, which opened in 2013. The Carrie Nation is on the block next to the Massachusetts State House on Beacon Hill, one of the forty-six locations where the Eighteenth Amendment to the Constitution that banned alcohol was ratified. Around the corner, there's a bar across from the State House known as the Twenty-first Amendment, which alludes to the Constitutional Amendment that repealed Prohibition. It is next to the apartment building where John F. Kennedy lived when a bachelor.

There is fascination abroad as well. "Taking inspiration from America's Prohibition era," the London Town webpage reported in 2014, "London is currently brimming with elusive bars hidden behind unmarked doors and unassuming entrances. With cocktails in teacups, suave jazz and glamorous dress codes, they invite those in the know to intimate yet raucous evenings. So, dust off your dancing shoes and dig out your map as London invites you into an underground world of illicit drinking."

The trend seems to have been first spotted in 2009 when the trade magazine *Restaurant Business* noted the seemingly counterintuitive strategy of marketing an establishment by making it hard to find, but that's what is being done by a growing number of bars and lounges. "Modern-day 'speakeasies,'" the magazine reported, "don't put up any signage, have unlisted phone numbers, require passwords and are often found behind secret entrances down shadowy alleys. Just as New York was the speakeasy capital during Prohibition—epitomized by the 21 Club—the modern trend began there but the phenomenon is spreading to other cities."

"Today's speakeasy is the bar as cinema," was one explanation given in the magazine *Art Culinare* in 2010. "It invites customers to become actors in a flickering movie from a nostalgic part of our collective history. Like the forbidden allure of an opium den, the modern speakeasy is a lush and dreamy stage of punched tin ceilings, dark wood paneling and potions swirling in glasses made luminous by the velvet light of flickering candles. Atmosphere is not the twenty-first-century speakeasy's only enticement. The drinks featured tended to be of the period harking back to a time when sipping a Manhattan, Bronx, or a Mary Pickford carried with it the titillating risk of getting caught."[1]

Coinciding with this came the aromas and flavors of the Dry Years. Bathtub gin and raw rye whiskey from tidewater stills were reincarnated as small-batch gins and ryes. Bitters and high-end tonics and mixers were coming into play finding new markets.

The quality of life around the bar improved when speakeasies reemerged a few years back. Food editor Devra First wrote in *The Boston Globe* in August 2014: "The trend has brought us better bartending and ingredients; it has restored to prominence delightful drinks we seldom got to enjoy and birthed plenty of new ones."

Conveniently overlooked in this neo-speakeasy movement is the fact that the new joints feature drinks made with high-end liquor coddled by "craft" bartenders who work hard to create cocktails that often start at twelve dollars a pop. As Felicity Cloake wrote in a critique of the modern speakeasy in the *New Statesman* in 2011: "Far from the heyday of mixology that some sources claim, this was a period in which cocktails were nasty, brutish and short." Among other sources Cloake cites is Frank Shay, who wrote in *Esquire* magazine in 1934, the year after Repeal: "The basic raw materials then available—and I use the term 'raw' advisedly—made it imperative that they be polished or doctored or decorated . . . in order that they might pass to their true goal without too great distress to the drinker."[2]

Meanwhile, the same urge that has given us the twenty-first-century speakeasy has also given us a revival of interest in shakers, hip flasks, and the hardware trappings of Prohibition. Walk into any Pottery Barn and you'll find a Speakeasy Collection inspired by the vintage barware of the era. And men's clothier J. Crew offers a speakeasy hip flask with the come-on: "Channel speakeasy-era panache with our leather-bound flask, a throwback to the heyday of discreet drinking."

Amazon.com offers dozens of hip flasks, including one described as a "Personalized Engraved Cross, Jesus, Christian 12 Oz Stainless Steel Pocket Hip Drinking Flask for Men and Women," as well a four-ounce flask hidden inside the cover of a Holy Bible—novelties that would have been most offensive to those elders of the Protestant denominations of the Prohibition Era who sought to have all references to wine expunged from both the Old and New Testaments by turning the references of wine to grape juice.

Reminders of the era abound in popular culture, where the Dry Years have their own solid niche, having given rise to a generation of romantic "characters"—the flapper, the private eye, the organized crime boss, the corrupt enforcer, the bootlegger, and the rumrunner—who live on in various media. Not only, for example, does *The Great Gatsby* hang on into the present, but it has been made into four Hollywood films (1926, 1949, 1974, and 2013) and one made-for-television film (2000).

There is even an emerging archaeology of Prohibition as entrepreneurs seek old speakeasy sites to be given new life. In 2013—the eightieth anniversary of Repeal—a collaboration between Preservation Detroit and the Wayne State University Department of Anthropology uncovered the existence of an illegal Prohibition-era speakeasy beneath Tommy's Detroit Bar & Grill at 624 3rd Street. It was rumored that the original speakeasy had ties to the infamous Purple Gang and other underworld organizations. Also in 2013, the *Dayton Daily News* reported that it had discovered the existence of an unusually decorated basement room in an East 3rd Street commercial building, which fits the long-running local legend about a hidden piece of downtown's Prohibition Era history. This room was part of a network of speakeasies reachable through underground steam heating tunnels crisscrossing downtown.[3]

But before the cocktail hour arrives, let us take a look at the subject through the prism of one real character—a bone fide bootlegger—named George L. Cassiday, remembered by the color of his fedora. Perhaps more than any other single individual, he served to exemplify and, ultimately, undermine the folly of the era.

Contraband
COCKTAILS

1

INTRODUCING
"THE MAN IN THE GREEN HAT"

Since the early days of the District of Columbia, people fretted about the drinking habits of its residents. The concern went beyond the intoxicated themselves. It was reasoned that if drunkenness were tolerated in the Capital, a hideous example would be set for the rest of the nation. So for more than its first 125 years, Washington was the initial target and prospective model for those who hoped to rid the nation of ardent spirits and their attendant ills.

Temperate people had legitimate cause for alarm. From its beginning as the new seat of government, Washington was a place where one was never more than a short walk from a stiff bolt. It is telling that the first recorded trial in the District was one in which a man named Jacob Leap was convicted of a liquor law violation. That was in 1801, when the city got its first drinking establishment, Rhodes Tavern. Within a few years,

250 new ones were in operation, which worked out to roughly one for every ninety residents.

By all accounts, early Washington was not only a hard-drinking community but one where there was scant appreciation for the weaker or subtler spirits. An English novelist visiting Washington in 1838 wrote in his diary that when one visits a Washington restaurant and "asks for pale sherry they hand you gin; brown sherry and it's brandy; Madeira—whiskey."

Drinking was rampant inside and around the Capitol building itself. Things reached such a state by 1833 that a committee of one hundred Congressmen and appointed officials took a public pledge of abstinence and immediately began plumping for a ban on liquor sales under the Capitol dome itself. The Senate banned liquor selling on its side in 1837, but it took the House seven more years to do the same.

Over time, those who would ban or restrict liquor sales gained in number if not strength. New groups were founded, church leaders became more active in the movement, and the city soon had its own large meeting place and monument to those who had taken *the pledge*. In 1843, the cornerstone was laid for Temperance Hall on the south side of E Street NW between 9th and 10th. (The building housed the Freeman's Temperance Society and survived on the spot until shortly after Prohibition ended and was finally razed.)

Periodically, local groups united with national groups based in Washington and would attempt to get Congress to impose some form of prohibition on the powerless city. They met with little initial success, which is not to say that they did not make their presence known. A great prohibition parade staged on February 14, 1907, marched up Pennsylvania Avenue, stormed the Capitol, and demanded and got an impromptu hearing. The pressure became a constant as the marches, rallies, and lobbying continued.

As the nation as a whole moved towards prohibition, it was all but inevitable that the District of Columbia would be pushed into prohibition early to serve as an example. The power required to impose prohibition on the federal city came through passage of the Sheppard Act, a special law introduced by Senator Morris Sheppard of Texas. Under this law, it became effective on November 1, 1917, more than two years before the rest of the country came under the Eighteenth Amendment and the enforcement power of the Volstead Act. Under the provisions of the Sheppard Act, the last of 269 legal retail liquor stores and bars within the confines of the city were shut down at the stroke of midnight.

Although the police were told to be prepared for fighting, rowdyism, and rioting, the night on which prohibition came to Washington was relatively peaceful, remarkably cheerful, and unquestionably noisy. Thousands thronged Pennsylvania Avenue and the other downtown streets where there were a number of saloons. Everything liquid was being sold either for immediate consumption or "take out," and the more resourceful came downtown with wheelbarrows and pushcarts. It was also Halloween, and the idea had gotten around that costumes were in order to give the evening the look of Mardi Gras. The area's barroom singers came out in force, addressing the question of "Where do we go from here?" and sometimes answering with "Over there." For all its horrors, the free-spirited, booze-tolerant, European War zone took on sudden appeal as midnight drew closer.

Along "Rum Row"—the saloon-heavy area on and around F Street near the Treasury—many of the neighborhood's more serious drinkers were not only out to say goodbye to John Barleycorn (at least in his legal incarnation) but to pay their respects to such institutions as Shoemaker's, the Ebbitt, Hancock's, and Denis Maloney's. Most of the places in this part of town began running dry about 10:00 p.m. and started to close early. At the Ebbitt where there was nothing left to drink but water at 10:45 p.m., something remarkable happened that was not soon to be forgotten: several loyal customers who had feared such a moment unpacked precious private supplies of liquor, which were used to restock the bar. At midnight, when the bars closed, some diehards headed off in the direction of Baltimore. A mere forty arrests were made during the night.

The first phase of the "Great Experiment" was underway, but it began to falter within minutes as several of the just-shuttered gin mills quickly reopened with slightly inflated prohibition prices in effect. A few months later, there were twice as many illegal establishments operating inside the District as there had been legal ones before the act was passed.[1]

During Washington's three-year head start on the rest of the nation, local residents learned how to spot a speakeasy, connect with a reliable bootlegger, and brew beer or fabricate gin at home. To the average middle-class Washingtonian, the cocktail hour was infused with new meaning and celebrated as a point of honor. "Folks seemed to imagine that if they didn't serve cocktails, other folks would think they were obeying the law, and such a thought, to a liberty loving people, was naturally unbearable. So people served cocktails under prohibition who had never dreamed of serving them in their own homes before,"

The Washington Herald recalled during the early days of the Sheppard era. "The grand fiasco of the prohibition experiment was already becoming apparent."[2]

With the District of Columbia serving as vivid testimony to the fact that Prohibition could not be enforced, Congress passed the Volstead Act or National Prohibition Act on October 28, 1919, over the veto of President Woodrow Wilson. The Eighteenth Amendment had been pushed through Congress in 1917, and at high speed through forty-six of the forty-eight state legislatures in 1918 and 1919; Connecticut and Rhode Island were the only two of the forty-eight states to vote against it. The Amendment allowed one last year of legal drinking, with Prohibition beginning on January 16, 1920. Never before had so many states ratified an amendment to the Constitution; the Anti-Saloon League of America was not immodest in calling itself "the strongest political organization in the world."

After the Eighteenth Amendment went into effect in 1920, one group that felt singled out and punished by the law were the veterans, still returning from France and the Great War in large numbers when it was passed. One man who felt this way was an outgoing twenty-five-year-old veteran named George L. Cassiday. Born in West Virginia of a mother who was a member of the Women's

"The Man in the Green Hat," George L. Cassiday.

Christian Temperance Union and a teetotaling father, his first taste of liquor was near the front during the War. He was still overseas when Congress passed the bill: "I believe my attitude toward Prohibition was no different than that of most of the American boys who went overseas. We saw liquor being used in all the allied countries and when we were at the front, detailed with French troops. I received rations of cognac along with the other men."

He served with the 321st Light Tanks, a heavily decorated unit that returned in late 1919 on a transport ship carrying 2,200 American troops. "We took a straw vote on Prohibition just before the ship docked in New York," Cassiday wrote. "All but 98 of the men aboard voted against it."[3]

George Cassiday soon had larger worries than Prohibition. When he returned to his home in the District of Columbia, he tried to regain a railroad job he had held briefly before going overseas. But he was turned down because of a physical disability he had incurred in France. He got married and entered the new decade without steady work. By the summer of 1920, when he had become desperate in his search for the means to support his family, Cassiday heard from a friend that good brand-name liquor brought top dollar from members of Congress who were no longer content with the novelty of corn liquor or "white lightning" easily trucked in from back-country stills of Maryland and Virginia. His friend insisted that somebody could make a decent living slaking the thirst of Capitol Hill. Two days later, that friend met him in a hotel lobby and introduced him to two members of the House of Representatives—both of whom had voted for Prohibition in 1919—who placed an order with him.

Cassiday was learning what the rest of the nation would

soon learn: congressmen and senators would be elected who voted Dry, drank Wet, and slept with a clear conscience. He obtained good liquor and was soon filling many Congressional orders, launching his illegal career. At the suggestion of a member of the House of Representatives, Cassiday set up a bootlegging operation inside the Old House Office Building. He had an office, storeroom, and lavatory—all supplied at taxpayer expense—and was soon serving scores of congressmen and their constituents, spending, as he would later brag, "more time there than most of the Congressmen."[4]

Soon he was making twenty to twenty-five deliveries a day to members of both houses, Republicans and Democrats, Drys and Wets. Because of the nature of the material he delivered and the need for discretion, he was given the keys to many Congressional offices. His first regular source of high-quality bonded liquor was an operation on Seventh Avenue near 34th Street in Manhattan, a source he was led to by a former agent of the Treasury Department, the agency in charge of enforcement.

After five years of smooth sailing, a sudden squall nearly capsized Cassiday's lucrative business. A Capitol police officer, whom Cassiday believed to be sympathetic, arrested him for delivering six quarts of whiskey to a House member. This so-called "Green Hat incident" received wide press attention, resulting in Cassiday being known as the Man in the Green Hat. The incident also prompted the House to ban Cassiday from the Old House Office Building (now known as the Cannon House Office Building). Undeterred, the bootlegger shifted his operations to the Senate Office Building (now the Russell Senate Office Building) and continued undisturbed for another five years from 1925 to 1930 when, under instructions from Vice

President Charles Curtis, a zealous and resourceful Federal prohibition agent named Roger Butts finally arrested him.

Cassiday was sentenced to eighteen months in jail, but he created a major scandal when he sold his memoirs to the *New York World* and *The Washington Post* in which, among other things, he said he had the keys to more Capitol Hill desks and offices than any person in history. In this memoir, Cassiday estimated that he was keeping 80 percent of the House and Senate in drink. "If they got a kick out of it with no bad side effects, they were well satisfied," he wrote. The initial series ran October 24–29, 1930. The final article ran exactly one week before the midterm election day.

In the persona of the Man in the Green Hat, Cassiday became a national symbol on two levels—as a symbol for the stunning hypocrisy of Prohibition, and also as the embodiment of the dilemma of the World War I veteran. The Man in the Green Hat was a disabled vet who got direct help from Congress, not because it was right, but because they were thirsty. "It is true that I served more Republicans than Democrats and more drys than wets," he proclaimed in his newspaper memoir, "but that was only because the Republicans and the drys have been an overwhelming majority in both branches of Congress during the period."

When Cassiday was forced to drop his profession in 1930, Congress still had many bootleggers working its halls and offices. Bootleggers were operating in front of police headquarters, in the Justice Department itself, and across the street from the White House. When *Washington Post* reporter Edward T. Folliard ducked out to buy a pint of gin from his favorite bootlegger, he found the supply had just run out. He jumped into the bootlegger's car and drove to the White House, where a large burlap bag was retrieved from the hedge. He took out a half dozen bottles of gin and returned the rest. The bootlegger told the reporter that the White House hedge was as safe a place as any to stash booze because nobody would expect anyone to hide their liquor there. Folliard told the story in a short whimsical *Associated Press* piece, unabashed that he had admitted his involvement in an illegal act.[5]

A citizen criminal class was, in fact, being created in Washington. In 1929, 5,217 were arrested for Volstead violations, and 14,056 under the much stricter provisions of the Sheppard Act—roughly one of every twenty-seven District residents was arrested that year for alcohol-related incidents. Since all drinking was illegal, there was no legal drinking age and so no incentive to screen minors. Women who had not been welcome in the old saloons were accepted in the new speakeasies, and the local smart set hung out at places like Le Paradis on Thomas Circle. For this reason, the *Washington Herald* termed Prohibition the "hand-maiden of woman's suffrage, of equal rights—of the single standard."[6]

Atop the heap of illegal bars and restaurants in Washington was the Mayflower Club at 1223 Connecticut Avenue, reputed to be the swankiest speakeasy in the city during the Dry Years. It offered gambling as well as illegal booze, and catered to what was then called high society. The club featured a thirty-foot bar and was decorated in a Halloween motif. The murals on the walls focused on famous people playing jazz, so one could find likenesses of the teetotaling Irish playwright George Bernard Shaw tooting the clarinet and Mahatma Gandhi playing the piano. The speakeasy was enjoyed by the young social set of the city. Champagne was ten dollars a quart—that is, until the establishment was raided in November 1933, a month before Repeal.*

Prohibition had turned the Capitol City into a tragicomic melodrama where ironies, contradictions, and hypocritical behavior were occurring at such a rate that it took a really rich item to attract attention. A drunken policeman was no longer news, but the fact that Evalyn Walsh McLean, the fabulously rich heiress to a Colorado mining fortune and owner of the incomparable Hope Diamond, could brag that she had her whiskey—actually only the choicest liquor and best champagne—delivered to her Washington mansion by police escort was newsworthy, as were her lavish, zany, and boozy parties staged with her husband, *Washington Post* owner Ned McLean.[7]

Then there was the celebratory and widely advertised Bootleggers' Ball staged smack dab in the middle of Prohibition and held at the city's Auditorium. The enforcers showed up in force, led by the city's plainclothes police. As the *Washington Daily News* later reported, "The ball was a feint to get the highways leading into Washington uncovered, so that huge consignments of Baltimore and Jersey liquor could be run in."[8]

In 1977, a group of young investors opened a restaurant on Capitol Hill called the Man in the Green Hat, which survived for more than a decade. My wife and I were involved as part owners of the restaurant. The night before the restaurant opened, we were getting it ready and an elderly man knocked on the door. He identified himself as Roger Butts, the former

---

* Today the site is occupied by a spacious bar that pays homage to *The Mayflower*. It is called MCCXXIII—1223 in Roman numerals.

Treasury agent who had arrested George Cassiday in 1930. He let us know in no uncertain terms that we had chosen to name our restaurant after a man who had broken the law. In 2012, the first post-Prohibition distillery, New Columbia Distillers, began operating in Washington, D.C. Its first product was Green Hat Gin.

From the standpoint of the nation, the view of Prohibition in Washington would be all-important. In the end, it would provide the example that ultimately led to Repeal. In one important respect, Washington was fortunate in that Prohibition did not foster the violent gangsterism of other large cities. There were no gang wars, and no significant subclass was being created to support the liquor trade, as was the case in Chicago or New York City. There were few real heavies, let alone anyone approaching the outlaw status of "public enemies" on the order of Al Capone, Legs Diamond, or Dutch Schultz.

It was not all fun and games. In February 1924, Senator Frank L. Greene went out for an evening stroll on Pennsylvania Avenue with his wife. The couple walked right into a gun battle between a bootlegger and a Prohibition agent. The Senator was seriously wounded when a bullet hit him above the right eye. He survived, but more than a dozen bootleggers, several innocent bystanders, and at least one District policeman were killed before Prohibition was over. Many more people were injured in gunfights and car chases in and around the city.

Outside the Capitol, folks found they could distill their way out of the worst effects of rural poverty and ultimately the Great Depression. The "blessed day" was the name given to the day Prohibition was ratified. January 16, 1919, was the day in which some coastal areas were lifted to, as Fred Tilp put it in his history of the Potomac River, "glory and prosperity." Tilp alluded specifically to the tidewater lands of the Potomac, where small farms were turned into profitable wineries and distilleries. Local grain was used in making mash for whiskey stills. "Rye was the favorite," Tilp wrote, "followed by bourbon and corn."[9]

Making moonshine out in the country and selling it downtown was a largely colorblind pursuit. A policeman in a Virginia city was quoted in 1925: "White men used to get rich selling whisky to Negroes, but in these days the Negroes are getting rich selling whisky to white men."[10]

2

UNINTENDED CONSEQUENCES

Prohibition was responsible for a number of unintended consequences, including acting as the catalyst for the rise of organized crime and a culture in which bootleggers and rumrunners were often more admired than reviled. The most successful bootleggers—as represented by F. Scott Fitzgerald's fictional Jay Gatsby—accumulated great wealth, which granted these men entrée into high society.

Marni Davis points out in *Jews and Booze: Becoming American in the Age of Prohibition*: "Urban ethnic criminal occupations of the past, like arson, pimping, and robbery, carried an ugly social stigma for all but those most desperate for a ghetto-based model of ethnic self-esteem. Prohibition-era bootleggers, on the other hand, were often glorified rather than marginalized in urban society. The "glamorization of bootlegging," Davis adds, made gangster culture seem chic and attractive to other young and ambitious urban Americans. "Gangster slang and style became a subject of fascination and emulation in popular culture, a development that obscured distinctions between moral and immoral behavior." Suddenly, jail became the *big house*, someone killed by the mob was *bumped off*, detectives were *gumshoes*, and a criminal lawyer was a *lip*.[1]

Rumrunners posed and were accepted as heroes and patriots. None fit the bill as well as Captain Bill McCoy, known far and wide as "the real McCoy." As the King of the Rum Runners and founder of Rum Row, he compared himself to John Hancock and other patriotic smugglers of colonial times. In his own account of his exploits, McCoy suggested that Hancock, who ran cargoes of liquor and other illicit commodities into the American colonies, "might stand as the patron saint of rumrunners."[2]

A teetotaler himself, McCoy nevertheless fueled the Roaring Twenties by smuggling more than one million bottles of illegal alcohol from the Caribbean to New York. McCoy's maritime daring and willful defiance of the unpopular Eighteenth Amendment and government authority made him a household name during the era and earned him a Robin Hood–like mystique with the American public—one that has survived into the twenty-first century. He was the "hero" of a 2012 American Public Television documentary and was a recurring character in *Boardwalk Empire*. Unlike others of his ilk, McCoy dealt in unadulterated spirits, giving rise to a new meaning for the old phrase for the genuine article, "the real McCoy."*

---

* Despite many claims to the contrary, the phrase "the real McCoy" was in common use with the same meaning decades before the birth of Bill McCoy. Eric Partridge in *From Sanskrit to Brazil* (1952), says that it dates from the 1880s and originated in Scotland, where it was applied to whisky, men, and things of the highest quality. The whisky was exported to both the United States and Canada, where people of Scottish origin drank the whisky and

McCoy was not alone as a provider of high-grade liquor or the only rumrunner to pen a memoir. In September 1923, Scotsman Alastair Moray set out from Glasgow to the United States on board the 187-foot, four-masted schooner *Cask* loaded with thousands of cases of fine Scotch whiskey. It took Moray months to sell his cargo, a feat detailed in his book *The Diary of a Rum-Runner*: "A great deal of the whisky sold here reaches the consumer as it leaves us, that is, if it is going to one of the good clubs, first-class hotels or any of the wealthier homes or good restaurants; all of them have their own private bootlegger or firm of bootleggers, who deliver the proper goods."

Among the rumrunners were a handful of women who belied the long-held assumption of the Prohibitionists that women would stand as one in the fight against booze. The most notorious was an operator who called herself Spanish Marie, who took over her husband's ship when he fell overboard in 1926 after excessive sampling of his cargo. She cut an image of a female pirate as she strutted about with a revolver strapped to her waist, a big knife stuck in her belt, and a red bandanna tied about her head. Spanish Marie was captured in March 1928 while unloading liquor on the beach at Coconut Grove near Miami, and was released on $500 bail on the

---

kept the phrase alive. That said, Bill McCoy certainly popularized the term. As Herbert Asbury wrote of him in *The Great Illusion*: "He bought and sold his own booze, sometimes in partnership with wholesalers in Nassau and in this country, but he had no tie-ups with the big bootleg syndicates and was notorious along Rum Row for selling good liquor and dealing fairly with the purchasers. He often boasted that he handled nothing but 'the real McCoy.'"

plea that she must go home and take care of her babies. The bail was increased to $3,500 when investigators found the children at home with a nurse while Spanish Marie was drinking at a speakeasy. The record doesn't show that she was ever tried.[3]

3

GOTHAM

Prohibition fostered the emergence of tens of thousands of speakeasies, or "blind pigs." "Clip joints" and illegal night clubs far outnumbered the legal watering holes—mostly saloons—that had been closed the night Prohibition went into effect. These illegal places were everywhere, but it was along the Atlantic Seaboard from Boston to Baltimore and Washington that the Wet spots merged into a continuous belt, and here was the real focus of hostility to the Eighteenth Amendment. New York City was the epicenter of resistance to Prohibition. As journalist Pete Hamill pointed out in his introduction to *The Speakeasies of 1932*: "The gaudy saga of Prohibition has generated an extensive literature, of course, but in New York, the story has a special, almost personalized vehemence. From the beginning, millions of citizens felt that the national movement to make drinking illegal was directed at cities in general, and New York in particular. Most New Yorkers believed that the anti-booze people were a combination of right-wing rural politicians, severe (when not addled) Protestant clergyman, and feminists who unjustly linked Prohibition to the just cause of women's suffrage."[1]

A map prepared in 1924 by Mrs. Mabel Willebrandt, assistant attorney-general, showed the degree of non-enforcement in different sections of the country to vary from 5 percent in Kansas, Utah, and Idaho, to 95 percent in New York City.[2] By 1929, Police Commissioner Grover Whalen could tell *The New York Times*, "Nowadays all you need is two bottles and a room and you have a speakeasy. We have 32,000—in contrast there are 4,200 restaurants operating in all five boroughs." At one point during Prohibition, the Danish firm of

A crowded bar in New York City, the night before Prohibition went into effect. June 30, 1919.

Georg Jensen reported that it was selling more of its cocktail shaker sets in Manhattan than in the rest of the world combined.

Manhattan was the Wettest of the boroughs. The great concentration of illegal booze was in the city's "white light district," which stretched from 14th Street to 59th Street along Broadway and two to three blocks on either side. Humorist Robert Benchley once walked the north and south sides of 52nd Street between Fifth and Sixth Avenues, and counted fifty-eight speakeasies. Texas Guinan, Manhattan's most famous speakeasy hostess, managed more than half a dozen joints herself in or near the district, including the 300 Club, the Texas Guinan Club, the Century Club, Salon Royale, Club Intime, and the Club Argonaut.

The establishments within the white light district generally catered to a class of drinker who wanted the "good stuff," and the price of a glass of uncut Scotch of high quality ranged from fifty cents to a dollar a drink. A May 1925 *New York Herald-Tribune* report on conditions along Rum Row pointed out that even after a recent attempt by the Coast Guard to cut down on waterborne deliveries, the only thing in short supply was champagne, but that you could get just about anything else you wanted. The better speakeasies boasted of expansive wine lists.[3]

In New York and other major cities, there was, as historian Preston William Slosson during the period called it, "a curious and almost comical inversion of class relations . . . Instead of Lady Bountiful visiting the slums to redeem the drunkard, the slums were now shocked at the conduct of the gilded youth." A janitor's wife in New York asserted, "It's not our people that are drinking so much. It's the rich bums that come from outside . . . It used to be some lively down here before Prohibition, but that was our own people and you could say to them, 'Jim, you go along home to Maggie 'till you get sobered up.' But these rich bums, you don't know where to tell 'em to go." After studying conditions in Massachusetts, Dr. Richard C. Cabot of Harvard declared: "The rich may, for all we know, be as foolish as ever, but beyond any question the poor are better off."[4]

The other irony is that the saloon had been mostly driven from the major cities. Saloons had become ubiquitous, aided in large part by new technology. As Hugh F. Fox testified in 1919 as secretary of the United States Brewers' Association: "The invention of artificial refrigeration practically doubled, or more, the capacity of the breweries, and the result was an enormous over-competition and tremendous increase in the number of saloons. The result of that over-competition was, as you gentlemen of course have observed, in all our large cities, a very much greater number of saloons than were needed for the reasonable convenience of the people." The very same technology that had aided the saloon was a boon to the speakeasy where ice was the essential cooling agent for all cocktails, coolers, and mixed drinks.[5]

New Yorkers, in the meantime, witnessed an unparalleled show on and off shore as the Prohibition agents and the Coast Guard took on the battle to stop illegal imports. *The Times* (London), of May 9, 1925, reported that the U.S. Federal Government was making a most determined effort to enforce Prohibition. Off New York, for one hundred miles along the coast, it was maintaining a virtual blockade of the so-called "Scotch Armada," the new name for the rum fleet. Every rum vessel was surrounded by government vessels, so that in three days not a drop had reached the shore. Seaplanes were being used in patrolling, it was said.[6]

The Manhattan speakeasies, in the words of the newspaperman Stanley Walker, "contributed more than anything else to the madhouse that was New York." The speakeasy had become a symbol to New Yorkers who saw it as a patriotic institution. "I predict the day," wrote newspaper columnist Louis Sobol in 1935 shortly after Repeal in *Hearst's International Magazine*, "when the New York speakeasy will shine on the pages of history, niched in honor beside the Boston Tea Party."

The illegal sites provided a fertile ground where jazz and swing flourished. The male "crooner" and the female "songbird" styles of singing gained a foothold there. Nightclubs displaced legal cabarets and thrived on payoffs to Prohibition agents and police and with the support of organized crime. The best example was Harlem's Cotton Club. In his autobiography, *Of Minnie the Moocher and Me*, Cotton Club jazzman Cab Calloway explained that Prohibition was indirectly responsible for his becoming a star because it allowed him to get his big break in Harlem. As Calloway explained: "The underworld saw to it that there was booze all over the country in those days, but there was more of it in Harlem, just like there was more and better music in Harlem in those days. The Jazz Age in Harlem. Hell, jazz grew up in Harlem after it left New Orleans and Chicago . . . Harlem was swinging."

Calloway added that those were the places where high-society white people came to hear jazz, and where, during most of those years, "Negroes weren't allowed in the audience. They were okay on the stage or in the kitchen, but not in the audience. Well, those white people came uptown to hear the music but they also came to drink."[7]

At the high end, these clubs were elegant places with white tablecloths and elegant décor. "On Friday nights in the smart clubs, people dressed black tie or white. You saw top hats everywhere," recalled renowned restaurateur Toots Shor in a 1958 interview. During Prohibition, Shor had been a bouncer in several Manhattan speakeasies (The Five O'Clock Club, The Napoleon Club, and Maison Royale, among others). "Despite reports to the contrary," Shor added, "the whiskey was good in the good speakeasies."[8]

4

THE RISE OF
THE COCKTAIL CULTURE

Less well known—or appreciated—is the fact that Prohibition also begat, on a large scale, the rise of the cocktail and the custom of the cocktail party. To be sure, the cocktail was an American invention with roots in the culture of the earliest days of the Republic. "In the department of conviviality the imaginativeness of Americans was shown both in the invention and in the naming of new and often highly complex beverages," wrote H. L. Mencken in *The American Language: An Inquiry into the Development of English in the United States*, which was created at the very start of the "Dry Error."[1]

Cocktail parties were virtually unknown and without a name until Prohibition. *The Oxford English Dictionary* finds the first appearance of the term in print in 1928 in D. H. Lawrence's *Lady Chatterley's Lover*: "She almost wished she had made her life one long cocktail party and jazz evening."[*]

Malcolm Cowley observed in 1931 that the cocktail party "conceived as a gathering together of men and women to drink gin cocktails, flirt, dance to the phonograph or radio and gossip about their absent friends, had in fact become one of the most popular American institutions; nobody stopped to think how short its history had been."[2]

The new order of things had put the gentlemen-only saloon and hotel bar out of business, and what replaced it was a new cocktail culture where women drank with men. Frederick Lewis Allen, writing *Only Yesterday* in 1931, had still fresh in his mind the image of "well-born damsels with one foot on the brass rail, tossing off Martinis." Reporter Elmer Davis in *Harper's Magazine* wrote: "The old days when father spent his evenings at Cassidy's bar with the rest of the boys are gone. Since Prohibition, mother goes down with him."[3]

Members of the well-entrenched status quo not only consumed bathtub gin but also produced it. The great cook, food writer, and confessed scofflaw James Beard was one of them: "The mother of two girls I knew decided that she would go into bathtub gin production rather than worry about the safety of bootleg gin for her daughter and their friends. She enlisted the services of some of us, and Sunday afternoons were spent making gin in the bathtub, then rolling it around the floor in a wooden cask to 'age.' Several hours later it was served in our

---

[*] Recently, this has been challenged by a writer from *The Wall Street Journal* who found an earlier use of the term, but the *Oxford English Dictionary* has stuck to its guns and still lists *Lady C.* in its online edition. Besides, it makes for a better story.

Sunday night's cocktails. I may say that after two years at this I became deft as a gin maker."[4]

Along with what some have termed the Cocktail Age came a certain style complete with sleek chrome cocktail shakers, snazzy portable bars, Art Deco–styled bar tools, and streamlined cocktail carts. This design style was featured in a 2011 exhibition at the Rhode Island School of Design, *Cocktail Culture: Ritual and Invention in America 1920–1980* (which was quickly nicknamed "swizzle and sizzle"). The silver cocktail shaker became the ultimate symbol of the era with the greatest status attributed to those from big-name designers like Norman Bel Geddes and Raymond Loewy. A reporter for the *Evening Star* named William Johnson writing from New York on Christmas Eve, 1922, observed that what was odd about Christmas shopping this season was the brisk trade in cocktail shakers: "In every store at the counter where these were displayed was a long line of waiting customers." As the reports of sales of shakers and flasks from New York and other big cities grew, so too did small-town America do its part. "Even in the smaller towns and villages the windows of the jewelry establishments and the novelty shops have been filled with articles of this character," revealed a front-page article in the *Star* two days later, which also discussed elaborate monogrammed leather portable medicine chests meant to carry quart bottles of liquor.[5]

The shakers came in all shapes and styles, including one modeled after a fire extinguisher often placed in speakeasy windows to tip off tipplers. During the 1928 Christmas shopping season, several sporting goods stores in Midtown Manhattan reportedly featured an automatic iceless cocktail shaker "for the tired businessman."

The shaker was a byproduct of Prohibition, pure and simple. "When plain and fancy bar-room drinking was in flower no one had ever seen in a saloon a silver container with a lid on top and a spout sticking out the side," George Ade wrote in his 1931 classic *The Old-Time Saloon*. Ade posited his own theory on the emergence of the shaker: "Probably one explanation is that synthetic stuff has to be chilled to the limit and whipped to a lather, in order to get rid of the liniment taste and make it resemble something to drink."[6]

But the shaker and the cocktail went together like hand in glove. The only reason one needed a shaker was to make a cocktail. On the other hand, a mixed drink or highball required, at most, a swizzle stick and a paring knife to carve out a strip of lemon peel or bisect a lime. Over time, the strict line between cocktail and mixed drink—between that which is to be shaken and that which is to be stirred—have blurred, with many restaurants listing mixed drinks under cocktails on their menus.

Moreover, there was a ritual that went along with the shaker that involved vigorous action. "Shake the shaker as hard as you can; don't just rock it; you are trying to wake it up, not send it to sleep," advised bartender Harry Craddock. "This is the only way in which cocktails may be iced thoroughly; no amount of stirring will achieve the same result." Craddock was an American who fled the United States during Prohibition and became the bartender at the American Bar at the Savoy Hotel in London in 1920. He invented a number of cocktails and was most famous for making the dry martini one of the most popular drinks of the era.

The shaker also had a deeper significance, as Andrew Sinclair put it in his book on Prohibition: "For the working classes, as a whole, rightly regarded the practice of prohibition as a piece of class legislation, which deprived them of their beer while allowing other classes full freedom of the cocktail shaker."[7]

When British writer G. K. Chesterton visited a Dry America in 1921, he noted: "No steps are taken to stop the drinking of the rich, chiefly because the rich now make all the rules and therefore all the exceptions, but partly because nobody ever could feel the full moral seriousness of this particular rule. And the truth is, as I have indicated, that it was originally established as an exception and not as a rule." Other foreign visitors were alternatively appalled and amazed. On a visit to New York in October 1922, Sir Arthur Conan Doyle, no stranger to sleight of hand, reported: "I have seen a lady produce a cocktail in the course of a dinner as if it were a conjuring trick."[8]

Along with the raccoon coat, the shaker was an essential prop for the big man on campus—especially at those institutions that catered to the sons of wealthy. The Eastern institutions were the Wettest, or at any rate the frankest about their Wetness. As late as 1928, 110 incoming Princeton freshmen admitted that they drank. The anathema to the Dry forces was Yale University, which was not only in a state that was determinedly lax in enforcing Prohibition but where the campus ethos was soaking Wet.*

The absence of a shaker also held a symbolic value. Behold Sinclair Lewis's vacuous, conformist George F. Babbitt, who eschews the shaker but loves his cocktails. To quote from *Babbitt*: "Besides the new bottle of gin, his cellar consisted of one

---

* Your attention is directed to the Yale cocktail at the end of the Formulary on page 134.

half-bottle of Bourbon whisky, a quarter of a bottle of Italian vermouth, and approximately one hundred drops of orange bitters. He did not possess a cocktail-shaker. A shaker was proof of dissipation, the symbol of a drinker and Babbitt disliked being known as a drinker even more than he liked a drink. Instead of a shaker he used an old gravy boat and creates cocktails of his own image of what one should be—kind of a Bronx and not yet like a Manhattan is how he described one of his 'fine, old cocktails.'"[9]

The other piece of essential scofflaw hardware was the pocket flask. In his 1922 report on Christmas shopping in New York, William Johnson of the *Star* also reported a booming trade in hip-pocket flasks of all sorts. "There is nothing unusual, of course, in picking a gift of this sort for a man," he reported, "but when a father the other day showed me a flask he had bought as a Christmas gift for his daughter, it certainly seemed like a commentary on the changing times." Flasks were sold in every imaginable variation, including those sold that doubled as belt buckles, flasks encased in heavy leather that were advertised as being able to survive a taxicab crash, and rib flasks able to hold a quart or two. But there was more: hollow walking canes that could store a quart of booze, and jackets and overcoats with immense pockets one writer called "portable saloons."

As the state of Indiana banned both cocktail shakers and hip flasks and other jurisdictions made it harder to buy drinking accessories, the more the sales of such accessories flourished, the more store windows became loaded with products demanded by a drinking public. No place was this trend more common than in Midtown Manhattan, and at no time was it as overwhelming as during the Christmas shopping season. On December 16, 1928, Tom Pettey of the *Chicago Tribune* filed a dispatch from New York that said in part: "The store windows are loaded with byproducts of the dry law, and the carol singers of yesterday are buying silver cocktail shakers. Santa Claus is going into the bootleg accessory business and Manhattan is going to make a pagan festival out of the Yuletide." Pettey's report was of a city gone crazy over the cup that cheers. Printers worked overtime to produce Christmas greeting cards with appropriately Wet

A woman pours liquor from a hollow cane into a cup at the soda fountain.

mottoes and verses. A canvas of some of the larger station-ary shops reveals that 50 percent of their products contained some reference to liquor, bootlegging, or Prohibition.

Secondhand furniture dealers became bar caterers on the side. Tom Pettey, who was fascinated with the logistics of Prohibition, also wrote: "Now one can rent a bar for the evening, the weekend or season and have it delivered to the apartment from the van along with bartender, apron, dirty towel and everything." Nostalgia for the bygone saloon had become rampant among sophisticates who had never set foot in one, and there was a major market in place for pre–Volstead era nudes and other wall hangings as well as secondhand brass rails and cuspidors that were suitably dented.[10]

Beyond the booze was the food that went along with the cocktail party. Finger food became fashionable, which helped to increase liquor tolerance by ensuring that partygo-ers weren't drinking on an empty stomach. Along with this came the cocktail sausage, the cocktail napkin, the cocktail onion, the cocktail tray, the cocktail dress, cocktail attire, and much more.[11]

During the driest days of Prohibition, the cocktail hour itself took on special significance with those who infused it with its own grace, charm, and significance. In the *Clinical Notes* section of the September 1924 *American Mercury*, edited by George Jean Nathan and H. L. Mencken, there are comments on the cocktail that end with a semireligious take on the cocktail hour as the most charming time of the day: "Work is done, and relaxation looms ahead. The factory whistles are losing themselves in the strumming of guitars . . . The cocktail baptizes the evening. And the evening slides down the runway, smoothly, gracefully, into the rippling sea of music and laughter and banter and love and heart's ease."[12]

There was, of course, a dark side to all of this as a visit to a cocktail party or a speakeasy became, as Andrew Sinclair put it in his book *Prohibition: The Era of Excess*, "[a] sign of emancipation, a Purple Heart of individuality in a cowardly and conforming world." Sinclair adds: "Perhaps one of the greatest crimes of prohibition against the middle classes was to make public drunkenness a virtue, signifying manliness, rather than a vice signifying stupidity."[13]

In many circles, there was constant pressure to consume large numbers of cocktails. Novelist Joseph Hergesheimer made headlines when he boarded an ocean liner for Europe in September 1932 because it was a place "where a man doesn't have to take a drink unless he wants to." His claim was that he was hounded by friends "forcing" him to drink gin cocktails, which he hated (but he did like whiskey and claret.)[14]

By the end of the 1920s, enforcement was spotty at best. A store called Cordials & Beverages opened in early 1930 at 201 East 44th Street, offering liquor and wine. The store was painted orange and green as if advertising its scofflaw identity. *Time* magazine chronicled the store's trade week by week, and even published a letter from a man from suburban Bronxville stating that the strength of the gin sold there for a dollar a quart was exceptional, adding: "I hope this shop will be permitted to continue operation, as I have to pay $2.00 for gin in the delicatessens in Bronxville and Tuckahoe, and $2.50 in the Wall Street district."

As in the rest of New York, booze in Harlem was sold all over the place—in speakeasies, under the table, behind the counter—everywhere. In his autobiography, Cab Calloway explained: "The federal agents who were sent around to enforce the act were, in my experience, mostly out for bribes. Once they got their money they would turn their backs. What Prohibition did do was place liquor under the control of the underworld gangs. And as long as the underworld controlled liquor, they controlled a number of clubs in Harlem as well. The cops knew damned well what was going on, but they were on the tab, from the precinct captain to the flatfoot on the beat."[15]

The fourteen Dry Years were also a prime time for the invention of new cocktails, often created by American bartenders driven out of the country as their profession became illegal. A case in point is the Bloody Mary, which was invented in the early 1920s by an Ohio-born bartender named Fernand "Pete" Petiot at a bar in Paris that would be later known as Harry's New York Bar.

Meanwhile, the exiled American masters of the cocktail became beloved figures. Harry Craddock went from Manhattan (where he served his last legal drink at the Hoffman House on Broadway) to London, where he presided at the Hotel Savoy and where he authored the *Savoy Cocktail Book*. He had a devoted and nationwide following in Dry America. In 1926, the *Atlanta Constitution* ran an exclusive story about him in which he was quoted on the desire of the exiled bartenders of America "scattered between London and

Shanghai, Bombay and Buenos Aires" to pack their shakers and come home. The article in the *Constitution* ends with a list of the 280 cocktails—from the Alexander to the Zaza—he was mixing at the Savoy. The list did not include the coolers, daisies, fizzes, flips, highballs, punches, sours, and rickeys he mixed in London.[16]

5

THE COCKTAIL AS ART
AND ENTERTAINMENT

As a distinctly American drink, the cocktail has a long-established role in American literature. As early as 1851, a character in Nathaniel Hawthorne's *The Blithedale Romance* is known for his skill in compounding gin cocktails (which appeared to be his sole talent) as a preamble to his dinner parties. In 1852, William Makepeace Thackeray published his novel *The Newcomes*, in which a character, a sea captain, describes the New York City custom of having brandy cocktails before dinner.[1]

The Dry Years were among the most fertile for literature about contemporary life and mores, especially in the United States, where cocktails appeared in a great many major works of the major writers. This was, after all, the time of *The Great Gatsby*, which at its most literal level was a book about Prohibition awash in mixed drinks, including the mint julep Daisy concocts for Tom at the Plaza Hotel toward the end of the book—"Open the whiskey, Tom," she ordered, "and I'll make you a mint julep. Then you won't seem so stupid to yourself . . . Look at the mint."

Then there is the cocktail in Fitzgerald's *This Side of Paradise*. About a third of the way into the book, the protagonist Amory Blaine makes some gains in losing his innocence at a New York nightspot. Encouraged by a chorus-girl companion, Axia Marlowe, he orders a double daiquiri and has a "inexpressibly terrible" vision of a man with a face like yellow wax. It is the devil himself. In *Tender Is the Night*, the gin and tonic has a cameo appearance: "At three he called Rosemary and was bidden to come up. Momentarily dizzy from his acrobatics, he stopped in the bar for a gin-and-tonic."

Fitzgerald was so obsessed with the cocktail that he suggested it ought to become a verb. He drew up a chart displaying all of its cases, including:

> IMPERFECT = I was cocktailing
>
> PERFECT = I cocktailed (past definite)
>
> PAST PERFECT = I have cocktailed
>
> CONDITIONAL = I might have cocktailed
>
> PLUPERFECT = I had cocktailed

Sinclair Lewis delighted in creating characters who supported Prohibition but who, like the narrator in *The Man Who Knew Coolidge* (1928), was not "a fanatic" about it:

> If a fellow feels like making some good homebrewed beer or wine, or if you go to a fellow's house and he brings out some

hooch or gin, but you don't know where he got it and it isn't any of your business, or if you have a business acquaintance coming to your house and you figure he will not loosen up and talk turkey without a little spot, and you know a good *dependable* bootlegger that you can depend on, then that's a different matter, and there ain't any reason on God's green earth that *I* can see why you shouldn't take advantage of it, always providing you aren't setting somebody a bad example or making it look like you sympathize with lawbreaking.

No sir![2]

Then there is Ernest Hemingway (there are martini-drinking scenes in both *A Farewell to Arms* and *The Sun Also Rises*) and other major Jazz Age writers—to name a few, John Dos Passos, John O'Hara, H. L. Mencken, Theodore Dreiser, and Edna Ferber.

Dashiell Hammett's characters Nick and Nora Charles in *The Thin Man* spend much of their time in speakeasies or hotel rooms toasting each other. Their drink, naturally, is the dry martini, and Nick is first spotted in the film version of *The Thin Man* instructing a bartender in its preparation: "A Manhattan should be shaken to a fox trot, the Bronx to a two-step, but a dry Martini must always be shaken to a waltz." Nora, waking up the next morning with an ice pack on her forehead, asks what hit her. "The last Martini," says Nick.

Beyond *The Thin Man*, the movies were soaking Wet. "The plot of the first all-talking motion picture revolved around bootleg whiskey," John C. Burnham says about *Lights of New York* (1928) in *Bad Habits: Drinking, Smoking, Taking Drugs, Gambling, Sexual Misbehavior and Swearing in American His-*

tory. Burnham added that an analysis of films released in 1930 revealed that drinking played a role in four-fifths of them and none of them depicted drinking in a truly negative light.[3]

Some films that seemed to have an anti-alcohol theme were, in fact, satirical. The purest example is the 1933 W. C. Fields classic *The Fatal Glass of Beer*, which mocks the moralistic tone of some early movies and older anti-drinking temperance shows. Fields was to become one of filmdom's chronic comic drunks. " 'Twas a woman drove me to drink," he slurred on occasion. "I never had the courtesy to thank her." He was not the first. Charlie Chaplin in *City Lights* (1931) and Buster Keaton in *What No Beer* (1933) were prime examples. Both Chaplin and Mary Pickford had period cocktails named after them.

If Hollywood was awash in booze, so too was Broadway, which had a similar fascination for the martini. The drink seemed to have restorative powers when inserted in song lyrics, such as Cole Porter's "Babes in the Woods," first performed in the *Greenwich Village Follies of 1924*:

> They have found that the fountain of youth
> Is a mixture of gin and vermouth.

In the end, the writers and filmmakers were leaders in the fight against Prohibition. For H. L. Mencken, Prohibition was the ultimate violation of the individual liberties he cherished. He wondered aloud and in print what George Washington would have thought of the Eighteenth Amendment—or Jefferson, particularly, for Virginia went dry before the rest of the country. As Marion Elizabeth Rodgers points out in *Mencken: The American Iconoclast*: "Mencken read reports of officers waking women passengers on sleeping cars and searching their suitcases, pawing through their underwear for contraband liquor. 'Imagine it! Virginians doing that! Try to imagine Jefferson's comment on it.' Such indignities meant that civilized people had to submit to a form of espionage 'by great hordes of shoddy and dubious men, each with full legal right to harass decent citizens.' It was one of the most cynical violations of the Bill of Rights he had ever witnessed." Mencken, who openly rejoiced as attempts to enforce the law failed, later recalled in his essay "The Noble Experiment" only two isolated instances during the entire period—1920 to 1933—when he could not find a drink if he wanted one.[4]

In organizational terms, the leader of the Wet writers and artists was a journalist and novelist named Irvin S. Cobb. He was a major celebrity in his time, close to the film community because of his screenplays and the host of the 7th Academy Awards in 1935. Not only did Cobb inveigh against Prohibition in his literary works, he made it a personal crusade. Joining a national organization called the Association Against the Prohibition Amendment, he became the chairman of its Authors and Artists Committee. Under his vigorous leadership, the committee ultimately boasted 361 members, including some of the nation's best-known figures. As chairman, he blamed Prohibition for increased crime, alcoholism, and disrespect for law. "If Prohibition is a noble experiment," he said, "then the San Francisco fire and the Galveston flood should be listed among the noble experiments of our national history."

Ten years before Repeal, Governor Gifford Pinchot of Pennsylvania gave a speech in which he bluntly identified the element that does most to obstruct enforcement: "It is not the solemn ass who gets up in assemblage and solemnly announces that 'pro-hibition cannot be enforced.' It is not the flappers and 'sheiks,' who rather take to the idea that it is clever and devilish to break the law. I don't mean those, either, of permanently immature minds who seem to be congenitally incapable of thinking there is anything more sacred than a cocktail before dinner. These folks do some harm, but not much . . . The real harm is done by able, influential people of the community who set themselves on the side of the bootlegger and against the law. All that is necessary to straighten them out is to have them come to a realizing sense of what they are doing."[5]

While deep in the Great Depression, the nation spent an estimated $36 billion on bootleg alcohol, and the government had collected not a penny of this amount in excise taxes. The jobs and revenue that legalized drinking brought with it were an immediate benefit of Repeal.

Once again bars were legal and operated under rules set by states and localities. Three years into the Noble Experiment, writer Ring Lardner had noted that the biggest difference in bars was that because, by law, there weren't any, they didn't have to close at any particular hour. "Now," he added, "they have closing times again."[6]

6

REPEAL AND THE GREAT CELEBRITY COCKTAIL CONTEST IN CARMEL-BY-THE-SEA

Repeal officially took place on December 5, 1933, at 4:31 p.m., ending 13 years, 10 months, 19 days, 17 hours, and 32.5 minutes of Prohibition. "What America needs now is a drink," declared President Franklin D. Roosevelt at the end.

The Great Celebrity Cocktail Contest was the brainchild of one John Callin, who had become weary of his San Francisco law practice and left—with tongue deeply implanted in cheek—to become the village blacksmith in the romantic town of Carmel-by-the-Sea, California. When he "discovered" that there was not a single horse within the limits of the town, he ran for mayor and was elected. When it became clear that Repeal was at hand, Callin formed a group called the National Association for the Advancement of the Fine Art of Drinking and issued a call for original drink recipes to be mixed and tasted on December 5, 1933, at the swank Hotel Del Monte in Carmel.

The drinks to be featured in the contest were mostly over the top and often self-referential. For example, Theodore Dreiser called his drink "An American Tragedy," and Sinclair Lewis's was called "Main Street Punch" (he said that if you drink two of these, you "won't be able to walk down Main Street"). Recipes contributed by former Del Monte guests and invited celebrities also included Edgar Rice Burroughs's Tarzan Special and the Marx brothers' concoction for Honeymoon Punch, with its parenthetical note that "one of these and the honeymoon is over." Newspapers covered the buildup to the tasting. No record remains of who actually won, but the contest did serve its purpose, which was to celebrate the liberation of the cocktail and the end of the Noble Experiment.

Shortly after the Carmel contest was over, a local printer published a booklet containing some of the recipes. Titled *Cocktail Recipes Mixed by Famous People for a Famous Hotel*, it became an important document leading the way to an avalanche of post-Prohibition mixing guides—some good, some bad.

7

THE ARCHAEOLOGY OF
THE COCKTAIL

About twenty-five years ago at a flea market in Florida, I found a very small six-ring binder with a black cover containing scores of typewritten drink recipes. It was, according to the man who sold it to me, a notebook created during Prohibition, when even books on mixing alcoholic drinks were seen as violations of the spirit of the law, if not the actual law. In *The American Language*, H. L. Mencken alludes to several pre-Prohibition bartenders' manuals and then notes: "The sale of all such books, I believe, is now prohibited, but they may be consulted by scholars in the Library of Congress."[1]

I enclose a sample of the typewritten manual on the next page.

This little black book fascinated me and introduced me to the idea of a book on drinks mixed during Prohibition— perhaps even appropriating a few of the recipes from it. I've now done considerable research into Prohibition-era cocktail making. One of the first things I learned was that cocktail manuals were not prohibited by statute but rather by practice

in those places where enforcement was most Draconian. The typewriter and the fountain pen became a more convenient means of passing along the secret to a perfect sidecar or a best way to manufacture bathtub gin.

While there was a reluctance to publish new cocktail manuals, there were several such books published in Great Britain, Cuba, and Canada and then imported into the United States, but only deep into the Dry Years. The most famous of these imports was *The Savoy Cocktail Book*, published in London in 1930 and authored by Harry Craddock.

Drink books were published in America during the period but were mostly privately printed—often crude affairs on the order of the little black book. I have found only a single example of a book for mixing drinks published in the United States by a mainstream publisher, and it is as much a cookbook for canapés to be served with specific drinks. This book, by Dexter Mason, published in 1930, was called *The Art of Drinking— or What to Make with What You Have (Together with Divers*

Succulent Canapés Suitable to Each Occasion). It was immediately reviewed by H. L. Mencken in the *American Mercury*. He deemed most of the recipes repulsive. Mencken asks of one of the drinks featured in the book: "Can you imagine any civilized man starting dinner with the thing Mr. Mason calls (apparently without conscious irony) *The New Yorker*?" The New Yorker was composed one part gin, one part lemon juice, two tablespoons of sour orange marmalade, and the white of an egg, all of which was to be shaken thoroughly before plenty of cracked ice is added and then frappéd.[2]

Then there are those extremely rare books and booklets that were either privately printed or published in extremely small quantities. Probably the rarest and most desirable is a small work titled *Bottoms Up—52 Cock-Tail Spins for High Flyers from the Recipes of Many Celebrities*, which is so rare in its original form that *Good Spirits News* reported in 2013 that only two copies are known to exist, and one of them recently sold for a hefty sum. The book was recently reprinted by Redowa Press and, among other things, contains recipes for the favorite cocktails of George Gershwin and W. C. Fields—the Silver Fizz and the Clover Club, respectively. The publisher was George Buzza, a major manufacturer of greeting cards.

My own oddest and scarcest find came recently when I obtained a second gem of scofflaw mixology. This was not a typescript like the first, but a privately printed American book published in March 1930 titled *My New Cocktail Book* by G. F. Steel. The book is so rare that I cannot find a copy in any library, including the Library of Congress or the New York Public Library, nor have I been able to find any copies offered for sale. This book contains a fascinating array of odd cocktails whose life appears to have begun and ended with the book's publication. Under the letter *L*, for example, we have the League of Nations, Loftus, Logan, Lone Tree, Los Angeles, and the Lusitania (named for the British ocean liner sunk by German U-Boats in 1915), which is a mix of ⅔ French vermouth, ⅓ "good" brandy, a dash orange bitters, and a dash of absinthe. Another of the letter *L* drinks is the Logan, which is ⅓ gin, ⅓ rum, and ⅓ milk.

In terms of cocktail archaeology, the single most valuable resource is *Manhattan Oases*, published on January 1, 1932; it was reprinted in 2003 as *The Speakeasies of 1932*, with a new introduction by Pete Hamill. The book contains drawings by caricaturist Al Hirschfeld, best known for his black-and-white portraits of celebrities and Broadway stars. The text, by Hirschfeld and writer Gordon Kahn, describes an array of working speakeasies. In their research, the two men went from the lowest dive to the fanciest establishment, which was then known as Jack and Charlie's—but later and down to the present is known as the 21 Club or just 21. The book also included recipes. "I interviewed all the bartenders, and the bartender would give me his favorite cocktail," Hirschfeld recalled in an interview just before his death at age ninety-nine. He added: "The one on the Bowery had a recipe for a drink called smoke, made with Sterno. I don't know how anybody survived it." *The Speakeasies of 1932* is an invaluable fly in amber, especially when determining what drinks were actually served.[3]

Ironically, if cocktail manuals were suppressed during Prohibition, there was a boom in books on how to make wine that—as a sop to the farmer—was deemed to be a legal activity. One of the most popular was a book published in 1909 titled *Old Time*

Recipes for Home Made Wine by Helen S. Wright, which was repeatedly republished during Prohibition. The book contains a few grape-based wine recipes, but its strength comes in showing the reader how to make wine from elderberries, gooseberries, raspberries, juniper berries, lemons, oranges, raisins, turnips, the sap of the birch tree, and something called scurvy-grass. There are recipes for both tomato wine and tomato beer, several dozen brandy recipes (including one made with poppies), a liqueur called Elephant's Milk, and instructions on how to make beer and ale from pea shells.*

In addition to the manuals themselves, drink recipes were

---

* The book has one of the most compelling introductions of any work I have encountered during my research. It began as she visited some widowed friends:

> The idea of compiling this little volume occurred to me while on a visit to some friends at their summer home in a quaint New England village. The social customs of this Adamless Eden were precise and formal. As with the dear ladies of Cranford, a call was a very serious affair, given and received with great gravity, and had its time limit set with strict punctuality. Cake and wine were invariably served as a preliminary warning toward early departure. Here came in my first acquaintance with many varieties of homemade wines, over whose wealth of color and delicacy of flavor my eyes and palate longed to linger. Vulgar curiosity made me bold to inquire the names of a few; imagine my astonishment when graciously told that the gay dandelion, the modest daisy, the blushing currant, had one and all contributed their nectar to the joy of the occasion. Flattered by my interest, my gentle hostess broke strict rules of etiquette and invited me to linger, showing me rare old gardens aglow with flowers, fruits and vegetables that in due time would contribute to their store, and at parting various timeworn recipes were urged upon me, with verbal instructions and injunctions upon the best methods of putting them to test . . . With a gentle hand I tie my little bunch together and present you my bouquet.

passed along in other media, almost as if there was a race to publish recipes in a format other than a bound book. *Vanity Fair* told its readers in its April 1930 issue about a collection of thirty cocktail recipes embedded within a bridge score pad, which the magazine endorsed: "This Book-Pad Collection is worth a dollar." There was also a cocktail tray with the copyright date of 1931, measuring 19.75 inches by 13.5 inches and made of painted wood, with a paper list of vintage cocktail recipes. It is titled "John Barleycorn—his Mappe—A Guide To A Mixture Of Pleasantries." It has a nautical motif and gives the recipes for including all the common drinks of the time, but also such concoctions as Between the Sheets, Hell Raiser, and Stretcher. Shakers were often emblazoned with drink recipes. A chrome shaker recently sold at auction with recipes for Between the Sheets, Clover Club, Bronx, Manhattan, Dubonnet, Gin Rickey, Metropolitan, Pink Lady, Palm Beach, Side Car, Alexander, Tom Collins, Bacardi, Whiskey Sour, Martini, and New Yorker etched onto its sides.

If there was a reluctance to publish drink books during the Dry Years, there was no such reluctance after Repeal as distilleries and importers of liquor became legitimate once again and all the major American publishers rushed cocktail manuals into print. Simon & Schuster published a U.S. edition of the *Savoy Cocktail Book* just as Repeal went into effect.

8

COCKTAILS *VS.* MIXED DRINKS — THE BITTERS DISTINCTION

One thing that was common in these cocktail manuals and in bar menus before, during, and after Prohibition was the distinction between cocktails and mixed drinks. By common definition, a cocktail was not really a cocktail unless it had bitters. Without bitters, it was a mixed drink. The first published definition of the cocktail appeared in an editorial response in an 1806 issue of a periodical called *The Balance and Columbian Repository* of 1806: "Cocktail is a stimulating liquor, composed of spirits of any kind, sugar, water and bitters." To the present day, the *Oxford English Dictionary* defines a cocktail as "a drink, consisting of spirit mixed with a small quantity of bitters, some sugar, etc. orig. *U.S.*"

The definition that appears in *Webster's Third International Dictionary*, published in 1961, seems to have captured what in actual practice was considered a cocktail in the twentieth century: "A short iced drink containing a strong alcoholic base (as rum, whiskey, or gin) or occasionally wine with the admixture, either by stirring or shaking, of flavoring and sometimes coloring ingredients (as fruit juice, egg, bitters, liqueur, or sugar) and often garnished (as with a sprig of mint slice of lemon)." The definition was not strict, as vermouth could be inserted in place of the bitters still making it a cocktail. An ad that ran in *Vanity Fair, Life,* and other leading magazines at the time of Repeal proclaimed: "People are going back to civilized cocktails—Martinis, Manhattans—cocktails made of vermouth. Why vermouth? Because it fills the true purpose of a cocktail: to stimulate the appetite. Doesn't dull it as sweet drinks do. It is tart—tangy."

For reasons unclear, bitters lost their allure in the last quarter of the twentieth century with lone bottles collecting dust behind bars across the nation while American dictionaries quietly dropped the word from the definition of cocktail in new editions. Few home barkeeps could pronounce the name Angostura (*anga-stura*, not *angus-tura*) or had an explanation for why the paper label was oversize and rose above the curve of the bottle. (The ill-fitting label was a nineteenth-century mistake in ordering rather than a twentieth-century marketing gimmick.)

9

DUFFY'S ASTERISKS

At the end of Prohibition, one of New York's most famous bartenders, Patrick Gavin Duffy, assembled a manual called *The Standard Bartender's Guide*, which would stay in print for many decades. Duffy, as the bartender of Manhattan's Ashland House (Fourth Avenue at 24th Street) for some forty years, served drinks to famous folks like Mark Twain, Oscar Wilde, and J. P. Morgan, and he chronicled their favorites tipples in his well-regarded book. Duffy was the man who is given credit for the creation and naming of the highball in the year 1895. The name, according to the most commonly cited etymology, came from the practice of raising a ball on a pole as a signal for a train to speed up or maintain maximum speed. The implication was that the dilution of liquor in a highball allowed the drinker to drink faster and more efficiently.[1]

In the first edition as well as all subsequent editions (including one revised by James Beard, a tippler of some note, in 1966), Duffy issues a strong warning about some of the drink recipes that had been included among the more than nine hundred in the original formulary:

Most of the following extensive and carefully selected list of cocktails have been served over first class Bars in the United States, South America, Canada and Europe, since our Civil War. There are, however, a considerable number which were created here during the period of Prohibition 1917–1933 and some of these are obviously of irresponsible origin. During these years, the huge traffic in liquor was conducted by the inexperienced and lawless element of the nation and the great hotel, restaurant and legitimate saloon men who were the backbone of the business had absolutely no part in it. For this spirit of resignation and law-abiding behavior, the public did not accord due credit. The youth and many adults of the great cities, seeing they were forbidden a custom their fathers were free to enjoy, now took to the "Speak-Easy," and gilded Cabarets and the orgies which followed became more and more wild until finally those well-meaning persons who brought Prohibition on became alarmed and sought Repeal as eagerly as they had, two decades before, clamored for the "Dry Law."

Duffy then goes on to admit (as he would in all future editions of his own collection) that some of the "Cocktail Creations" of those hectic days were bad ideas. He then cautions barkeepers and others against adopting some of them for general use. He added that they were published as a matter of record and as a mirror in which future Americans could see the follies that the enactment of the Eighteenth Amendment produced. The drinks he disapproved of—and which included his asterisk of disapproval—included one drink in which gin, Scotch, brandy, vermouth, and cream were muddled together. He added: "Nor indeed, can we give our support to any concoction consisting of Gin and Rye, Gin and Scotch, Gin and Brandy or to any beverage where two kinds of strong liquor are included especially when they are 'shaken together with bitters, cream and Raspberry Syrup.'"

Over time as new type was set and as revised editions of Duffy's book were printed, the asterisks disappeared and terrible drinks like Alexander's Sister and the Cowboy Cocktail (⅔ Scotch and ⅓ cream, iced and strained into glass) began to appear along with the palatable ones. As others rushed to publish their own compilations, the Cowboy was dutifully copied and appears in such books as *The Old Mr. Boston Bartender's Guide, The Diner's Club Drink Book* (1961), *The Ultimate Cocktail Book* (1998), *The Ultimate A–Z Bar Guide* (1998), and *The Complete World Bartender Guide: The Standard Reference to More than 2,400 Drinks* (1993), among others. If one looks hard enough through old drink recipes put out by distillers, one can also find such variations as the Adios (essentially a Cowboy made with the addition of a teaspoon of strained honey and topped with grated nutmeg (from *The Art of Drinking*) and the Rum Cowboy (from a Sibony Rum booklet published in the 1930s).*

---

* The Cowboy Cocktail is one of those bad formulas that not only lost its *asterisk* but lives on in cyberspace where it is listed in a number of mixology websites, presented without warning.

Almost all the truly bad drinks cited by Duffy and others involved mixing liquor with milk or cream. As William Grimes put it in his history of the cocktail: "Prohibition launched a thousand alcoholic milk shakes that can curdle the blood even at a distance of sixty years."[2]

So it is that some of the worst concoctions of the Dry Years have survived. Duffy's asterisk-free editions are now long out of print, but they live on through a number of massive drinks collections on the internet.

Before moving onto the question of which drinks to include in my formulary, there is the question of what actually belongs there and what does not. The issue is more than purely academic, as many of today's faux speakeasies feature drinks that were yet to be invented at the time of Repeal. A case in point is the Zombie, which was a post-Repeal rum drink of three rums and tropical fruit created by a Don the Beachcomber in 1934, which became the signature drink of the 1939 World's Fair at Flushing Meadows. Another example is the Mai Tai, which cocktail historians have concluded was a 1944 creation of Trader Vic's.

In November 1933, the Mayflower Club, by all accounts the swankest of all the Washington, D.C., speakeasies, was raided and padlocked, and its proprietor hauled off to jail. The place was so well established that it featured an elegant menu that listed all seventeen cocktails and a similar number of mixed drinks. The menu was published several days later, and today serves as a guide to what was actually in vogue during the Dry Years. All the cocktails and many of the mixed drinks are included in what follows—albeit with some interpretation: a drink called a Dykeree is almost certainly a Daiquiri.[*3]

The cocktails listed on the menu are all in the formulary, with the exception of a drink called the Club Mayflower, whose formula has been lost awaiting rediscovery by some future cocktail archaeologist.

* The cocktails ranged in price from $.50 to $1.00.

10

THE FORMULARY—
AKA "LIBERTY'S LIBATIONS"

In the spirit of Duffy's asterisk, I have marked several of the formulas with a symbol ⊤ to signify that the drink is included for historic or literary reasons rather than as one that might be worthy of replication. The nonalcoholic cocktails are marked with the symbol §.

These formulae are presented as close to that which would have been employed at a high-end speakeasy or private home during the Dry Years rather than as an attempt to suggest the perfect incarnation of the drink. For example, if one enters "mint julep recipe" in the Google search engine, you get more than 500,000 hits; if you enter "the perfect mint julep," you get 126,000 hits. These are not all recipes, but the bulk of them are. As Abe Dobkin wrote in his *Home Bartender's Guide*: "There are almost as many versions of the mint julep as there are julep fanciers."

One should also be aware that during and immediately following Prohibition, recipes often carried measurements that are not common today. Here is the translation of measuring terms from William Guyer's *The Merry Mixer or Cocktails and Their Ilk: A Booklet on Mixtures and Mulches, Fizzes and Whizzes*, in what he termed "simple 1933 units":

> 1 dash equals ⅓ of a teaspoon
>
> 1 jigger equals 1½ ounces
>
> ¼ wineglass equals 1 ounce
>
> 1 wineglass equals 4 ounces
>
> 1 pony equals 1 ounce
>
> 1 barspoon equals 1 teaspoon[1]

ALEXANDER

⅔ jigger (1½ oz.) dry gin

½ jigger sweet cream

½ jigger Crème de Cacao

PREPARATION Shake well with cracked ice and strain into large cocktail glass.

VARIATION If brandy is used in place of gin, the name is changed to a *Panama Cocktail* or, more commonly, a *Brandy Alexander*.

CULTURAL CONTEXT Despite the fact that some people called this drink an abomination and worthy of one of Duffy's asterisks, the drink remained fashionable and popular. When Crosby Gaige published his *Cocktail Guide* in 1941, it made his Hall of Fame, composed of the handful of drinks whose composition in most households, restaurants, and grills "is as friendly and familiar as the formula for the baby's bottle." He added that the cocktails so honored had been tested and proven in such famous laboratories as the bars of the Waldorf, the Ritz, and 21 in New York, the Palace in San Francisco, the Ambassador in Chicago, and Alciatore's in New Orleans. Under his recipe for the drink, Gaige added the caveat: LADIES, WATCH YOUR STEP!

BACARDI

Introduced to American imbibers who traveled to Cuba during Prohibition, this drink became, according to Charles Columbe, the author of *Rum—The Epic Story of the Drink That Conquered the World*, the most popular of all speakeasy rum drinks. The problem was that the drinks were often made with other brands or inferior replicas of the real thing. One place that made the real thing was Tony's at 59 West 52nd Street in Manhattan, which was the bar of choice for the "vicious circle" of friends who populated the Algonquin Round Table. With members such as writers Dorothy Parker, Harold Ross (founder of *The New Yorker*), and Robert Benchley; columnists Franklin Pierce Adams and Heywood Broun, and Broun's wife, Ruth Hale; critic Alexander Woollcott; comedian Harpo Marx; and playwrights George S. Kaufman, Marc Connelly, Edna Ferber, and Robert Sherwood, the Algonquin Round Table embodied an era and changed forever the face of American humor. The group was dominated by scofflaws, but they did not drink at their luncheons as the owner of the hotel forbade it, fearing he could be shut down.

The Bacardi was the drink of choice offered by bartender Tony for *The Speakeasies of 1932*.

Juice of ½ lime

½ teaspoon powdered sugar

1 jigger (1½ oz.) Bacardi rum

Dash of grenadine

PREPARATION Place in mixing glass and stir thoroughly. Then add fine cracked ice and shake vigorously. Strain into cocktail glass.

CULTURAL CONTEXT The Bacardi cocktail has been the subject of a good deal of controversy over the years—i.e., is it a Bacardi when made with another brand of rum? The drink was the subject of a ruling by the New York State Supreme Court on April 28, 1936, that required the drink to be made with Bacardi rum in order to be called a Bacardi cocktail.

THE BEE'S KNEES

This cocktail got its name from 1920s slang that simply meant "the best" or "cool," along with a host of other parallel constructions, including "the flea's eyebrows," "the canary's tusks," "the cat's pajamas," "the snake's hips," "the dog's tuxedo," "the eel's ankle," "the elephant's in-step," "the snake's hip," and "the caterpillar's spats."

To make honey simple syrup: combine ½ cup of water and ½ cup honey in a small saucepan. Heat over medium, whisking often, till the mixture reaches a slow simmer

and the honey is liquid and smooth. Remove from heat
and cool to room temperature.

2 ounces gin

½ ounce lemon juice

¾ ounce honey syrup

PREPARATION Shake with ice, strain into a chilled
cocktail glass, and serve.

BETWEEN THE SHEETS

It is often asserted that this drink likely originated in
Harry's New York Bar in Paris in the 1930s, but it actually first shows up in print in the 1919 edition of Harry
MacElhone's formulary. It became very popular during Prohibition. The recipe is adapted from *Cocktails
and Wines*, a booklet produced by the Huyler's chain of
restaurants in 1934. There were sixteen Huyler's in New
York City, including six on Broadway (at numbers 170,
221, 270, 863, 2149, and 2577).

⅓ light rum

⅓ Cointreau

⅓ brandy

1 dash lemon juice

PREPARATION Shake well with cracked ice, then strain into a chilled cocktail glass and garnish with a twist of lemon.

CAVEAT This is one of the drinks that bartender Patrick Gavin Duffy printed with an asterisk, indicating a cocktail he "personally did not recommend."

CULTURAL CONTEXT David Wondrich puts this drink in context in his *Esquire* online cocktail guide: "The ancestor of all the Silk Panties, Slippery Nipples, Screaming Orgasms, and other ungodly concoctions that so titillate the Abercrombie & Fitch set, the Between the Sheets dates to Prohibition—when, frankly, the nation's moral fiber wasn't what it ought to have been. But then again, neither was the nation's liquor supply. Which led to perversions like this— smutty name, too much alcohol."[2]

BIJOU COCKTAIL

A Jerry Thomas original that was very popular during Prohibition.

1 dash orange bitters
4 dashes White Curaçao
4 dashes Green Chartreuse
½ glass dry gin
½ glass Italian vermouth

PREPARATION According to Knut W. Sundin's *Two Hundred Selected Drinks*, shake well, strain into a cocktail glass, and add an olive or cherry according to taste.

CULTURAL CONTEXT A recipe for the Bijou, along with other cocktails, was included in an article in *The Washington Post* in August 1930, titled "How to Throw a Sure-Fire Party." It was listed with two possible canapés: potato chips filled with chutney, and caviar and onion. The article showed how far mainstream American newspapers had come in thumbing their noses at Prohibition by 1930.[3]

BLACK VELVET

This drink was invented in 1861 at the Brook's Club in London. Prince Albert had died, and everyone was in mourning. The story goes that the steward at the club, overcome with the emotion of the occasion, ordered that even the champagne should be put into mourning, and he proceeded to mix it with Guinness Stout. The half-and-half combination of Guinness on the top and champagne on the bottom symbolized the black or purple armbands worn by mourners.[4]

During Prohibition, the drink was given new notoriety by New York Mayor Jimmy "Beau James" Walker, who consumed them at all hours of the day and night. Walker was generous with his money, often buying drinks for the reporters following him.[5]

> ½ flute champagne
>
> ½ flute Guinness Extra Stout

PREPARATION Pour the champagne into a clean/ polished and chilled champagne flute. Slowly top up the glass with the stout, being careful to ensure no overspill.

CULTURAL CONTEXT Somewhere along the line, this drink got the reputation as a hangover cure or a "pick me up" with an eye to alleviating the morning's sad condition. It is listed as such, for example, in *Esquire*'s 1949 *Handbook for Hosts*. Actress Tallulah Bankhead wrote in her biography: "Wracked with a hangover I do my muttering over a Black Velvet, a union of champagne and stout." But she is quick to add: "Don't be swindled into believing there's any cure for a hangover. I've tried them all: iced tomatoes, hot clam juice, brandy punches. Like the common cold, it defies solution. Time alone can stay it. The hair of the dog? That way lies folly. It's as logical as trying to put out a fire with applications of kerosene."[6]

BLOODY MARY

This drink was invented by Fernand "Pete" Petiot at Harry's New York Bar in Paris during the early 1920s (5 Rue Daunou—or, as ads in the Paris edition of the *New York Herald Tribune* reminded the reader, "Just remember 'sank roo doe noo'"). According to Petiot's obituary (he died in January 1975, in Canton, Ohio), he came upon the idea after being introduced to vodka in Paris in 1920. The original version was basically vodka, tomato juice, and salt and pepper. A customer suggested Petiot name it a Bloody Mary, as it reminded him of a woman named Mary who worked at the Bucket of Blood, a saloon in Chicago. After Prohibition, Petiot set up shop at the St. Regis Hotel in New York and perfected his recipe, briefly retitling it a *Red Snapper* (later the name for the drink with gin) to appease the more "delicate American sensibility." In America, conventional wisdom held that the drink was named for Mary Tudor, the staunchly Catholic daughter of Henry VIII and Katherine of Aragon who had more than three hundred heretics executed.

When the drink began to take off in America in the mid-1950s, it was commonly seasoned with Worcestershire sauce and/or Tobasco and/or horseradish. Somewhere along the way, bartenders started stuffing celery stalks into the drink along with celery salt olives, and wedges of lemons and limes.

The Bloody Mary—in its original form of tomato juice,

vodka, and salt and pepper—is easy to make and allows for infinite variations. Here is the basic modern version from the mid-1950s offered by Smirnoff Vodka in an ad claiming that the drink had been invented by entertainer George Jessel—a great advertising ploy, but a total misattribution that lives on via the internet.

> 3 ounces heavy tomato juice
> 1½ ounces vodka
> ½ ounce lemon juice
> 6 drops Worscestershire
> Dash of salt and pepper

PREPARATION Shake well with ice, strain, and serve.

CULTURAL CONTEXT The invention of the drink was dependent on the creation of tomato juice as a canned or bottled commercial product, which did not occur until 1917 and was not produced in bulk until the early 1920s. Canned or bottled tomato juice did not become popular in America until vodka became widely available around the same time. Not only are there innumerable variations on the basic recipe but offshoots as well, such as the Bloody Molly (with Irish Whiskey), Bloody Maria (with white rum), and Danish Mary (with Aquavit). There is also a version made with gin, which a few (including James Beard) insisted was the original, but the overwhelming evidence points to vodka.[7]

BLUE MONDAY

One of Harry Craddock's Prohibition-era classics from *The Savoy Cocktail Book*.

> 3 parts vodka
>
> 1 part Cointreau
>
> 1 dash blue vegetable extract food coloring

PREPARATION Shake with ice and strain into a cocktail glass. No garnish.

INSTRUCTIONS How to drink it? As Craddock advised, "Quickly, while it's laughing at you!"

BRANDY CRUSTA

In the nineteenth century, the "Crusta" was introduced as a drink that included a sugared rim and lemon peel extension of the glass as a garnish, giving it a citrus collar.

> Rind of ½ lemon cut into long strip
>
> 1 glass brandy
>
> ½ ounce lemon juice
>
> 1 teaspoon grenadine
>
> 3 dashes Angostura Bitters
>
> 3 dashes Maraschino
>
> Powdered sugar

PREPARATION Moisten the rim of a small wineglass with lemon juice, dip rim in powdered sugar to give glass a crusted appearance (hence *crusta*), peel the rind of ½ a lemon and use it to line the glass, fitting the contour of the glass. Then pour into a shaker the grenadine and the dashes of Maraschino and bitters, the juice of half a lemon, and one glass of brandy. Shake well. Pour into wineglass.

CULTRAL CONTEXT It was—and still is—regarded as a drink of pretention, which is why it comes as little surprise that this was the drink proffered by Eddie the chief barman in Al Hirschfeld's *The Speakeasies of 1932*, who served at the Mansion at 27 West 51st Street: "The most pretentious place in New York, or it will do until the most pretentious place is built. Luxury and pump with flunkies that work as fast and noiselessly as genii."[8]

BRANDY FLIP

In *The Speakeasies of 1932*, this drink is proffered by Tommy the bartender at Julius's in Greenwich Village, 159 West 10th Street, which Al Hirschfeld described as "A madhouse without keepers." By the time Hirschfeld visited the place, it had been closed and padlocked four times. There are many variations on this drink, including those that substitute whole cream for the egg yolk and others that use the whole egg. This was the recipe in *The Speakeasies of 1932*.

Yolk of fresh egg

1 teaspoon sugar

1 glass brandy

Dash of nutmeg

PREPARATION Shake well, strain into small wine-glass, and grate nutmeg on top.

CULTURAL CONTEXT The first bar guide to feature a flip (and to add eggs to the list of ingredients) was Jerry Thomas's 1862 *How to Mix Drinks; or, The Bon-Vivant's Companion*. In this work, Thomas declares: "The essential in flips of all sorts is to produce the smoothness by repeated pouring back and forward between two vessels and beating up the eggs well in the first instance the sweetening and spices according to taste."

BRONX

This was deemed the most popular cocktail of the Dry Years. As G. Selmer Fougner of the *New York Sun* put it in 1937: "Gin was of course available at every street corner, so to speak; orange juice was equally abundant, and no art was required in the mixture." The Bronx was bound to lose some of its popularity with Repeal when ingredients other than gin became available again. Fougner and others have given credit for the invention and naming of the drink to bartender Johnnie Solon, who created it at the Waldorf Astoria sometime shortly after 1900.[9]

As Solon explained to Albert Stevens Crockett in *Old Waldorf Bar Days*, the drink was created by a patron who challenged the bartender to come up with a new cocktail. The challenge was carried to Solon by a man named Traverson, the headwaiter of the Empire Room. The drink was concocted and given to Traverson to taste. He swallowed it whole and declared that it would be a big hit.

"The name?" Solon told Crockett. "No, it wasn't really named directly after the borough or the river so-called. I had been at the Bronx Zoo a day or two before, and I saw, of course, a lot of beasts I had never known. Customers used to tell me of the strange animals they saw after a lot of mixed drinks. So when Traverson said to me, as he started to take the drink into the customer, 'What will I tell him is the name of this drink?' I thought of those animals, and said: 'You can tell him it is a Bronx.'"[10]

The remarkable thing is that Solon never touched a drop of liquor, but he had the uncanny ability to create great drinks.

> 1½ ounces gin
> ¼ ounce dry vermouth
> ¼ ounce sweet vermouth
> 1 ounce orange juice
> Garnish: orange slice

PREPARATION Pour the ingredients into a cocktail shaker with ice cubes. Shake well. Strain into a chilled cocktail glass. Garnish with the orange slice.

CULTURAL CONTEXT The most dramatic example of the impact of a single type of cocktail was the Bronx, which along with the Manhattan and the Martini were the preferred drinks of home bartenders and the better speakeasies. In New York City, the Bronx was by all accounts the most popular of all, and New Yorkers were consuming a large number of oranges from Florida that were then reputed to produce more juice than those from California. On September 12, 1925, Stephen Harvey, the mayor of Palm Beach, was in New York and made a stunning claim: the Florida land boom was the result of the Bronx cocktail and the demand for juicy oranges. The boom began the demand for agricultural land and later the demand for residential property.

Bill W., the founder of Alcoholics Anonymous, would later trace the beginnings of his alcoholism to a Bronx cocktail that he consumed while stationed as an Army officer in a camp in New Bedford, Massachusetts. The drink was served to him by a patriotic hostess entertaining Bill and his fellow officers. "In those Roaring Twenties," he remembered, "I was drinking to dream great dreams of greater power." His wife became increasingly concerned, but he assured her that "men of genius conceive their best projects when drunk." This was all an illusion, and after Bill hit rock bottom he led himself and others to sobriety.[11]

BROOKLYN

This from the Swedish-American Line head bartender Knut W. Sundin's 1934 edition of *Two Hundred Selected Drinks*.

> 2 dashes Angostura bitters
>
> 2 dashes Maraschino
>
> ½ glass whiskey
>
> ½ glass Italian vermouth

PREPARATION Shake well and strain into a cocktail glass and add a cherry.

CULTURAL CONTEXT Though it lacked the universality of the Bronx or the Manhattan, there was a cocktail named after the borough that advertised that if it were separated from New York City, it would be the fifth largest city in America. It appears to have been a favorite on booze cruises leaving from the port of New York.

C

CHAMPAGNE COCKTAIL

The Champagne Cocktail is one of the few drinks that survived intact from the original 1862 edition of *How to Mix Drinks* by Jerry Thomas; it appears in *The Speakeasies of 1932* as a drink of choice of Harry at the Club Napoleon at 33 West 56th Street.

> 1 sugar cube
>
> 3 dashes Angostura bitters
>
> 5 ounces Brut champagne
>
> Garnish: 1 lemon twist

PREPARATION In a small glass or dish, soak the sugar cube with the bitters. Fill a chilled flute with the champagne and add the sugar cube. Garnish with lemon twist.

CULTURAL CONTEXT This was said to be Audrey Hepburn's drink of choice. It was also featured in the Truman Capote novella *Breakfast at Tiffany's* and in the movie in which Hepburn starred.

# CLOVER CLUB

Named for the Philadelphia men's club of the same name, which met in the Bellevue-Stratford hotel. The drink dates back to 1896 at the Clover Club of Philadelphia, where it was said to have been invented by teenaged bartender Ambrose Burnside Lincoln Hoffman. According to the *Waldorf Astoria Bar Book*, the drink became a staple of East Coast bars and hotels. The Clover Club was seen in this era as one of the all-time classics, right up there with the Manhattan and Old Fashioned. It was very popular during Pro-hibition, featured in, among other places, the Cotton Club.

> 1½ ounces gin
> ¾ ounce fresh lemon juice
> ½ ounce simple syrup
> ½ ounce Chambord or grenadine
> 1 egg white

PREPARATION Pour all ingredients into a cocktail shaker with no ice. Shake for about a minute, to emulsify the egg white. Keep a tight grip on the top of the shaker; the shaking of the egg white builds up a lot of pressure in the shaker, and the mixture will want to spill out. Your Clover Club should look rather frothy. Then you can add ice and shake it again. Strain your cocktail into a chilled long-stemmed cocktail glass. Crosby Gaige, who listed it in his 1941 *Cocktail Guide* as one of the Hall of Fame drinks, added: "Garnish with a four-leaf clover." Float a mint sprig on top, and you now have a Clover Leaf.

CULTURAL CONTEXT As rapidly as the Clover Club rose to the heights of fashion, so it also came tumbling down after Prohibition ended. In 1934, *Esquire* magazine cited it as one of the worst drinks of the Dry Years. But the drink hung on, and by 1941 had made enough of a comeback to be listed in the Hall of Fame section in Crosby Gaige's 1941 *Cocktail Guide* as one of a certain select group of cocktails that have won and kept a vast clientele, and through "some accidental adumbrations of aroma and flavor, these famous favorites have pleased the public palate, and so flow daily down millions of warmly devoted gullets." Also in the 1928 collection of celebrity recipes, *Bottoms Up*, it is picked by comic actor W. C. Fields as his favorite cocktail.

CORPSE REVIVER #2

So called by the great expatriate bartender Harry Craddock as a "hair of the dog" hangover remedy. There is a corpse reviver #1 which was long ago overcome in popularity with its revised version.

> 1 ounce gin
>
> 1 ounce premium orange liqueur
>
> 1 ounce Lillet Blanc
>
> 1 ounce fresh lemon juice
>
> 1 to 3 drops absinthe
>
> Garnish: Maraschino cherry

PREPARATION Wash martini glass with drops of absinthe. Discard or leave in the glass according to preference. Place Maraschino cherry in bottom of the glass. Combine remaining ingredients in a cocktail shaker with ice. Shake to blend, and chill. Strain into the glass over cherry garnish.

CULTURAL CONTEXT Even if Craddock didn't actually invent the drink, we remember it because of him. He gave the formula for it in his 1930s classic *The Savoy Cocktail Book*, where he suggested: "Four of these taken in swift succession will unrevive the corpse again."

CUBA LIBRE

This drink dates to Havana around 1900, after the Spanish-American War ("Free Cuba" being the battle cry during that conflict, which began and ended in 1898 and led to Cuban independence). It was especially popular during Prohibition because of the availability of colas.

½ to 1 lime

Ice cubes

2 ounces rum, preferably gold or dark (see headnote)

½ ounce gin (optional)

Coca-Cola, chilled

2 dashes Angostura bitters

PREPARATION Squeeze the lime half or halves into a Collins glass (to yield ½ ounce juice), then drop in the spent lime half. Add 3 or 4 ice cubes. Pour in the rum and gin, if desired, then fill with the chilled Coca-Cola. Add the bitters; stir briefly to incorporate.

CULTURAL CONTEXT This drink has been known to be mixed with this line from Spanish poet and playwright Federico García Lorca: "The only things that the United States has given to the world are skyscrapers, jazz, and cocktails. That is all. And in Cuba, in our America, they make much better cocktails."

DAIQUIRI

An American named Jennings Stockton Cox is widely acknowledged as having invented the daiquiri, naming it after the Cuban town where he concocted the first one in 1898. The man credited with introducing the drink to America was an American Navy Medical officer named Lucius W. Johnson, who got the recipe and took it back to Washington, D.C., and served it to the Army & Navy Club, where today there hangs a plaque honoring Johnson's contribution at the club's Daiquiri Lounge.[12]

> 1 jigger West Indies rum
>
> Juice of ½ lime
>
> 1 teaspoon powdered sugar

PREPARATION Shake with finely shaved ice and strain into cocktail glass.

CULTURAL CONTEXT The bartender Constantino Ribalaigua Vert perfected the daiquiri at a Havana joint called El Floridita, later known as the Cathedral of the Daiquiri. Each evening, Ribalaigua appeared behind the bar dressed in a white shirt, a bow tie, a stylish vest, and an apron—"like an acrobat making his entrance onstage," as one historian put it. Among those who flocked to El Floridita were Gary Cooper, Tennessee Williams, Jean-Paul Sartre, and

Ernest Hemingway (the greatest daiquiri fan of all time), who consumed them before, during, and after Prohibition.

(FROZEN) DAIQUIRI

The daiquiri itself predated Prohibition, but not the frozen version that was also the brainchild of Constantino Ribalaigua Vert, the bartender of the aforementioned La Floridita in Havana. All he did was change back to shaved ice and use a blender and—voilà—the frozen daiquiri was born.

> 2 ounces White Bacardi rum
>
> Juice of ½ lime
>
> 1 ounce (or slightly less) white Maraschino
>
> 10 ounces shaved ice

PREPARATION Mix in electric cocktail mixer for 1 minute. Serve in a cocktail glass a bell-shaped drinking glass usually having a foot and stem and holding about three ounces.

CULTURAL CONTEXT One of the regulars at Vert's bar was Ernest Hemingway, who wrote on the walls of another famous Havana watering hole: "My Mojitos in la Bodeguita, my Daiquiris in La Floridita." Crosby Gaige wrote in his 1941 *Cocktail Guide* that this was the formula used by LaFloridita.

⊤ DEATH IN THE AFTERNOON COCKTAIL

Ernest Hemingway's original concoction, about which he explained: "This was arrived at by the author and three officers of H.M.S. *Danae* after having spent seven hours overboard trying to get Capt. Bra Saunders' fishing boat off a bank where she had gone with us in a N.W. gale." His instructions appear in Sterling North's *So Red the Nose*:

- Pour 1 jigger of Absinthe into a Champagne Glass.
- Add Iced Champagne until it attains the proper opalescent milkiness.
- Drink 3 to 5 of these slowly.

CULTURAL CONTEXT *So Red the Nose* says of Hemingway:

It takes a man with hair on his chest to drink five absinthe and champagne cocktails and still handle the English language in the Hemingway fashion. But Ernest has proved his valor, not alone in his cups. Captain of the swimming team at Oak Park High School—first American to be wounded on the Italian front during the World War (with 227 individual wounds to his credit)—tossed by a bull in the streets of Pamplona while rescuing his friend Donald Ogden Stewart—deep-sea fisherman—big game hunter—and one of the first citizens of Key West. Hemingway could hold his absinthe like a postwar novelist."[13]

⏍ DEATH IN THE GULF STREAM

The recipe first appeared in print in Charles Baker's 1939 first edition of *Gentleman's Companion*, having been picked up two years earlier from Hemingway in Key West. Baker had gone to see Hemingway on his yacht, the *Marmion*, with the expressed purpose of gathering recipes from him, including one for raw conch salad, or souse. As the Death in the Gulf Stream is an uncommon drink with literary overtones, it seems proper to quote Baker directly in describing how to make this "picker-upper."

> Take a tall thin water tumbler and fill it with finely cracked ice. Lace this broken debris with 4 good purple splashes of Angostura, add the juice and crushed peel of 1 green lime, and fill the glass almost full with Holland gin . . . No sugar, no fancying. It's strong, it's bitter—but so is English ale strong and bitter, in many cases. We don't add sugar to ale, and we don't need sugar in a Death in the

Gulf Stream—or at least not more than 1 tsp. Its tartness and its bitterness are its chief charm. It is reviving and refreshing; cools the blood and inspires renewed interest in food, companions and life.[14]

CULTURAL CONTEXT This cocktail was a favorite drink of Ernest Hemingway, who seemed to have no end of favorite drinks.

E

EL PRESIDENTE

For several generations, the drink was the specialty of El Chico in Greenwich Village, New York City. Here is the recipe from the 1949 *Handbook for Hosts*, exactly the way that bartender George Stadleman made it at El Chico.

> ½ ounce orange curaçao
> ¾ ounce French vermouth
> 1 dash grenadine

PREPARATION Stir ingredients well with cracked ice, then strain into a chilled cocktail glass. It should pour a delightfully clear, deep orange color. Garnish with a twist of orange peel.[15]

CULTURAL CONTEXT The El Presidente earned its acclaim in Havana during the 1920s when legions of alcohol-deprived Americans descended on the city by air and sea. It was named in honor of Mario García Menocal, president of Cuba from 1912 to 1920.

F

FISH HOUSE RUM PUNCH

During Prohibition, the drink achieved notoriety as the libation ladled out of the punchbowl on New Year's Eve 1930 at the Century Association at 7 West 43rd Street in New York City. It became an issue in the U.S. Senate on January 30 of that year when Republican Senator Smith W. Brookhart of Iowa read a letter alleging that "real gin cocktails" and "Fish House Rum Punch" were served at this exclusive club. Brookhart, a fervent supporter of Prohibition, read the letter aloud on the Senate floor to support his argument that drinking in New York City was out of control, even in the establishment clubs. Senator Royal Copeland of New York asked if the Iowan had ever been to the Association. He was told no. The New Yorker replied, "I wondered because I can't get in there with a pickax."

Here is the recipe for the drink, sometimes known as the Boston Fish House Punch.

> 1 cup sugar
>
> 3½ cups water
>
> 1½ cups fresh lemon juice (6 to 8 lemons), strained
>
> 1 (750-ml) bottle Jamaican amber rum
>
> 12 ounces cognac (1½ cups)
>
> 2 ounces peach brandy (¼ cup)
>
> Garnish: lemon slices

PREPARATION Stir together sugar and 3½ cups water in a large bowl or pot until sugar is dissolved. Add lemon juice, rum, cognac, and brandy, and chill, covered, at least 3 hours. Put half-gallon ice block in a punch bowl and pour punch over it.

CAVEAT This drink is very powerful and aptly labeled "a punch." In *Esquire's Handbook for Hosts*, this warning is attached to the recipe: "The impact of this punch is guaranteed to knock Santa Claus's beard right off its moorings, or break your lease. If you so desire."

CULTURAL CONTEXT This drink dates back to Philadelphia in 1732 at the Schuylkill Fishing Company. This establishment was also known as the Fish House, a dignified gentlemen's society devoted to manly vices, such as cigars, whiskey, and the occasional fishing expedition. Fish House Punch became quite popular—even palatable to the ladies—and it is said that John Adams was so partial to it that it was often served at the White House (of which he was the first resident). It remained popular well into the twentieth century and was often served during the holidays.

FRENCH 75

This drink was created in 1915 at the New York Bar in Paris—later known as Harry's New York Bar—by Harry MacElhone and first recorded in *The Savoy Cocktail Book* in 1930. The original recipe called for gin, lemon juice, simple syrup, and some bubbles. A later recipe replaces the gin with cognac. The combination was said to have such a kick that it felt like being shelled with the powerful 75-millimeter field artillery gun. It is also called a 75 Cocktail, or Soixante Quinze in French. The French 75, the predominant light artillery piece used by the Americans, was manufactured by the French. The "75" referred to the 75-millimeter diameter of the shell. Experienced crews accurately delivered as many as fifteen rounds per minute, thus creating the 75's reputation for efficient power and precision. This recipe comes from *The Stork Club Bar Book*.

> 2 ounces gin
> 1 teaspoon powdered sugar
> Juice of ½ lemon
> Brut champagne
> Cracked ice

PREPARATION Pour all ingredients except the champagne into a flute. Top with champagne and serve.

CULTURAL CONTEXT Popular during Prohibition, the cocktail became the signature drink of Manhattan's Stork Club, a scene where mobsters (Frank Costello, aka the prime minister of the underworld) rubbed elbows with celebs (Frank Sinatra, Marilyn Monroe) and politicians (the Kennedys).

GEORGE'S SPECIAL

Signature drink at George's Place, a speakeasy located at 507 Lexington Avenue in New York City. "Plain, green baize on the walls" is part of the description in *The Speakeasies of 1932*, which also mentions "A few photographs, one of Sir Thomas Lipton drinking beer." George, we are told, was one of the best at his craft: "Expert, but not showy. He keeps his distance. He uses no green crème de menthe—only the white—a dash of it goes into almost every gin drink he makes."

2 ounces gin

1 ounce apricot brandy

1 ounce lemon juice

1 dash green crème de menthe

PREPARATION Shake well and serve in cocktail glass with cherry.

GIMLET

Born during American Prohibition, this drink takes its name from a small hand tool used to tap into barrels in which wine or beer was stored. The name is also used figuratively to describe something as sharp or piercing. It has been suggested that the cocktail may have been named for its "penetrating" effects on the drinker.

The first recipe to be specifically called a gimlet appears in a British bartending guide from 1922. The original recipe for this drink was stated in proportions.

> ½ ounce Coates' Plymouth Gin
>
> ½ Rose's lime juice

PREPARATION Stir, and serve in same glass. Can be iced if desired.

CULTURAL CONTEXT Raymond Chandler's 1953 novel *The Long Goodbye* helped to give this drink literary cache: "We sat in the corner bar at Victor's and drank gimlets. 'They don't know how to make them here,' he said. 'What they call a gimlet is just some lime or lemon juice and gin with a dash of sugar and bitters. A real gimlet is half gin and half Rose's Lime Juice and nothing else. It beats martinis hollow.'"

GIN DAISY

The speakeasy known as Jack and Charlie's was located at 21 52nd Street, and the presiding bartender was a guy named Bill, "a pleasant, agreeable fellow never guilty of making the drink taste too watery or too strong." When the authors of *The Speakeasies of 1932* asked him to come up with his favorite cocktail, he suggested the Gin Daisy—which he measured in proportions rather than exact amounts.

> ⅔ gin
>
> ⅙ Cointreau
>
> ⅙ lemon juice

PREPARATION Serve over cracked ice with fruit ornamentation.

CULTURAL CONTEXT Jack and Charlie's not only weathered all of Prohibition, but continues to the present under its current name, 21. The original owners Jack Kreindler and Charlie Berns and their families owned the place until 1985. It was here that many years later Al Hirschfeld told a writer for *American Heritage* magazine that he saw Mayor James J. Walker; Robert Benchley, Dorothy Parker, and Heywood Broun; a judge or two; and Police Commissioner Whalen drinking here. He added: "Jack and Charlie were wonderful hosts and served the best liquor in town, which they husbanded down below, hidden, so whenever it was raided, they

just locked up everything." The secret vault is still there, behind a two-and-a-half-ton brick-covered door opened by a slim piece of wire; today it is often booked for private parties. "21," Hirschfeld said, had "the novelty of serving really good food" and kept out "the riffraff, the curious, by charging outrageous prices—twenty dollars for lunch!"[16]

GIN RICKEY

In *The Speakeasies of 1932*, this is the drink of choice selected by Bob, the bartender at the Press Grill, which was located at 152 East 41st Street, near the largest of the city's tabloid newspapers. This seems most appropriate, as no other drink—or series of drinks, in the case of the Rickeys—has such close ties to the world of journalism as the Gin Rickey, or, as it is sometimes called, the Lime Rickey.

> 1 lime
> 1 glass gin
> Soda or seltzer water

PREPARATION Place a piece of ice in a tumbler. Cut a fresh lime in half and squeeze the juice in the glass. Add one glass of gin and fill balance with seltzer or soda water.

CULTURAL CONTEXT The Gin Rickey was

created at Shoemaker's in Washington, D.C., a popular hangout for newspaper folks along Newspaper Row, which was at a right angle to Rum Row. Both Rows flourished in the years after the Civil War and into Prohibition. Rum Row included the Lawrence Hotel, Tim Sullivan's popular bar, which sported a beer garden and Shoemaker's Tavern. George Rothwell Brown recounted that Col. Joseph Rickey, a St. Louis lobbyist and drinkmeister at nearby Shoemaker's Tavern, was the originator of the "Whiskey Rickey," composed of whiskey, Apollinaris water (sparkling water), and lime juice, later made with gin and called the "Gin Rickey."

There are many versions of the story, but the most often repeated involves a fruit vendor entering the bar on an especially hot night and Ricky grabbing a fresh lime. He then asked the bartender to create a drink using juice of the lime. The drink was later modified for gin and other liquors. As *The Washington Post* reported during the end of the 1894 Democratic convention: "The convention adjourned along about half past 2 o'clock this morning and from that time until long after daybreak there was great joy everywhere. The favorite joy producers were Rickeys of various makes and of various degrees of strength. There were gin Rickeys and whisky Rickeys and brandy Rickeys and every other kind of Rickey known to mortal man."

THE GIBSON COCKTAIL

A bestseller during Prohibition. From *The Professional Mixing Guide or How to Get Drunk Fast*, here's how it was made during the Dry Years and before it had a major role in *Mad Men* as a vodka martini with three cocktail onions on a toothpick.

⅔ dry gin

⅓ dry vermouth

3 small pearl onions

Twist of lemon (for oil)

PREPARATION Stir well in cracked ice. Strain into cocktail glass prepared with the onions.

CULTURAL CONTEXT It was said to be named in honor of American illustrator Charles Dana Gibson. This is probably false: there's no evidence the illustrator had any connection to the drink.

GRETA GARBO

Honorific cocktail for the Swedish actress Greta Garbo. It was one of the special drinks concocted by Knut W. Sundin, star bartender on the ships of the Swedish-American line and one of the drinks featured in his 1930 *Two Hundred Selected Drinks*.

> Juice of ½ lime
>
> 3 dashes grenadine
>
> 1 dash absinthe
>
> ⅓ Cointreau
>
> ⅔ Bacardi rum

PREPARATION Shake well and strain into a cocktail glass.

CULTURAL CONTEXT During Prohibition, movie heroes and heroines drank like fish and uttered boozy lines recalled decades later. When Greta Garbo made her speaking debut in 1930 in the film *Anna Christie*, she uttered these unforgettable words: "Gimme a whisky with ginger ale and don't be stingy, baby." It was post-Prohibition (1937) when Mae West, playing the charming Peaches O'Day in *Every Day's a Holiday*, introduced the famous line: "You should get out of those wet clothes and into a Dry Martini." The importance of Garbo and West during and after Prohibition were great. As Norman H. Clark noted in his book *Deliver Us from Evil: An Interpretation of American Prohibition*: "Women learned from Garbo how to embrace, how to express sexual anguish, how to dress, how to drink, and how to smoke. From Mae West they learned smartly and wittily how to defy convention. The Reverend John J. Cantwell, Catholic Bishop of Los Angeles, expressed a militant dismay when he saw that 'talking pictures' could actually 'teach' a 'philosophy' which could undermine 'the sanctity of the home.'"[17]

H

HANGMAN'S BLOOD

This drink had its literary debut in Richard Hughes's 1929 novel A *High Wind in Jamaica* as a compound of rum, gin, brandy, and porter. Hughes said of it: "Innocent (merely beery) as it looks, refreshing as it tastes, it has the property of increasing rather than allaying thirst, and so once it has made a breach, soon demolishes the whole fort."[18]

In the 1960s, British novelist Anthony Burgess described its preparation as follows: "Into a pint glass doubles of the following are poured: gin, whiskey, rum, port and brandy. A small bottle of stout is added and the whole topped up with champagne. It tastes very smooth, induces a somewhat metaphysical elation, and rarely leaves a hangover . . . I recommend this for a quick, though expensive, lift."

HIGHBALL

A family of mixed drinks that are composed of an alcoholic base and a larger proportion of a nonalcoholic mixer. The literature of the Dry Years is awash in highballs. For instance, a woman enters a speakeasy and orders a Highball in Dorothy Parker's "Big Blonde" (1930). *Esquire*'s 1949 *Handbook for Hosts* terms it the "high priest of all tall drinks," and though it requires nothing but liquor, ice, and water or soda, mixing one calls for a certain procedure.

PREPARATION Here is how it is done properly, according to guidelines prescribed in *Handbook for Hosts*:

- Use a tall glass—at least 12 ounces— preferably uncolored, definitely sparklingly clean, admirably narrow-mouthed so soda will not collapse ahead of schedule.

- Next, put in the ice—one very large or two normal cubes.

- Pour the liquor over the ice—Scotch, bourbon, rye, brandy as you will. The customary amount is a jigger (1½ ounces).

Only now pour in the very cold sparkling water to the desired height, usually four times the amount of liquor. Bubbles thrive on coolness, but rapidly melting ice downs them, so the soda must be pre-chilled in a refrigerator. Some prefer plain water rather than fizz in their highballs, but if you would please palates don't try to pass off the chlorine-clogged stuff that comes from the kitchen faucet. Use an alkaline-sided mineral water, or any purified bottled aqua—but *cold*.

In any case, avoid stirring with metal, which is supposed to "squelch" the bubbles. "If one of your guests is stir-crazy," our 1949 *Handbook for Hosts* advises, "give him a plastic or glass swizzle stick."

In any case, serve it up immediately.

CULTURAL CONTEXT H. L. Mencken wrote: "The English, in naming their drinks, commonly display a far more limited imagination. Seeking a name, for example, for a mixture of whiskey and soda-water, the best they could achieve was *whiskey-and-soda*. The Americans, introduced to the same drink, at once gave it the far more original name of *high-ball*."[19]

JACK ROSE

The Jack Rose was a pillar of basic cocktail-mixing knowledge during Prohibition. The origin of its name is disputed: some credit it to an early twentieth-century gangster named Bald Jack Rose, while others connect it to Jersey City bartender Frank J. May, who was also known as Jack Rose. With its American apple brandy base, aka applejack or Jersey Lightning, the Jack Rose was a featured cocktail at the Cotton Club. It cost $.75.

> 2 ounces Applejack (Laird's)
>
> 1 ounce grenadine
>
> ½ ounce lemon juice
>
> ½ lime juice

CULTURAL CONTEXT Featured in Ernest Hemingway's *The Sun Also Rises*—"Brett did not turn up, so about quarter to six I went down to the bar and had a Jack Rose with George the barman."

⊤ MAIN STREET PUNCH

Cocktail created by Sinclair Lewis for the Great Celebrity Cocktail Contest in Carmel, California, on the night of Repeal.

> Juice of six lemons
>
> ½ pound powdered sugar
>
> ½ pint brandy
>
> ¼ pint peach brandy
>
> ¼ pint Jamaica rum
>
> 3 pints sparkling water

PREPARATION Stir in large punch bowl with block of ice.

MANHATTAN

A signature cocktail of the Prohibition Era. The drink has improved since Prohibition when it was often made with sugar syrup or powdered sugar to blunt the taste of inferior whiskey. The recipe in Dexter Mason's *The Art of Drinking* calls for ¼ part sugar syrup or powdered sugar, but here is how it was made by those with access to better quality whiskey.

> ¾ ounce Italian vermouth
>
> 1½ ounce rye or bourbon
>
> 2 dashes Angostura bitters
>
> 1 Marischino cherry

PREPARATION Shake well with cracked ice and strain into cocktail glass. Top with cherry.

CULTURAL CONTEXT Both during and immediately following the Manhattan was one of the trio of most popular American cocktails, along with the Martini and the Bronx. Its allure was given an extra boost by a popular 1929 melodrama from Paramount called *Manhattan Cocktail*, which was advertised with the tag line: "Mix a beautiful girl with two men—one good, one rich. Add Broadway gaieties, heartaches and temptations and you have a tingling, refreshing style *Manhattan Cocktail*." When higher quality whiskey was widely available after Repeal, it seemed to be offered everywhere. A major holiday gift in 1934 was a Christmas Manhattan gift package containing bottles of vermouth, whiskey, and Maraschino cherries—which retailed for $1.98. That same year Agua Caliente racetrack in Southern California offered a special Manhattan made with eight-year-old "Special Reserve" Bourbon for $.25.

MARTINI

In *The American Language*, H. L. Mencken traced the martini to the year 1899 and the name on the Martini & Rossi vermouth bottle, but other explanations abound. Two other theories appear in Robert Herzbrun's *The Perfect Martini Book*: (1) that it was named for the town of Martinez, California, where it was first served; (2) that it was named for a British rifle, the Martini and Henry, because of its accuracy and kick. Peter Tamony, the great etymologist, holds to several variations, including that of a bartender in San Francisco who made a client a special drink to keep him warm on a trip across the bay: the bartender found that his client was headed to Martinez, and so named the new drink.[20]

The martini, popular during Prohibition, is a far cry from later versions. The martini of the Prohibition era was commonly made with two thirds dry gin and one third French, or dry vermouth, and served with a green olive in the glass. This was called a Dry Martini. Others had their own take on vermouth. Algonquin wit Robert Benchley, who took his martinis at the best speakeasies in Manhattan, gave his recipe as "gin, and just enough vermouth to take away that nasty, watery look."[21]

Here is the recipe offered in Dexter Mason's *The Art of Drinking*, published in 1930.

> 1 part gin
>
> 1 part French vemouth
>
> 1 dash bitters
>
> 1 olive
>
> 1 twist of lemon peel

PREPARATION Shake with ice and strain into long-stemmed glass. Add olive and lemon peel.

CULTURAL CONTEXT The martini became the cocktail of the Manhattan speakeasies, especially popular in those that catered to artists, writers, and bohemians—reason enough for Broadway columnist Walter Winchell to refer to them as "gintellectuals." The Martini also acquired a naughty sophistication, by opposing the moralists behind Prohibition with its high alcohol content. It became urbane and sleek, a city drink. In the meantime, glass makers mass-produced V-shaped glasses on a tall stem (so that the hand would not warm the cocktail), which immediately became associated with the drink and is still known today as a martini glass.[22]

As speakeasies encouraged the mingling of men and women in a way that saloons previously had not, the martini brought with it a whiff of Eros best reflected in these lines from Dorothy Parker:

I like to have a Martini,
Two at the very most.
After three I'm under the table,
After four I'm under my host.

(DIRTY) MARTINI

2 parts gin

1 part vermouth

1 teaspoon olive brine

Lemon twist

Cocktail olive

Rub the lemon twist around the rim of a chilled martini glass. Combine gin, vermouth, and olive brine in a cocktail shaker with ice. Shake and strain into the chilled martini glass. Garnish with an olive.

CULTURAL CONTEXT As a presidential drink, there has been no other with such a persistent presence as the martini—beloved of selected Democrats and Republicans. It all began with Franklin D. Roosevelt, who is credited with popularizing what is today known as the Dirty Martini—dirty because of the addition of olive brine. He drank them with some regularity, mixing them in a silver cocktail shaker etched with the outlines of palm trees, and served them to many guests, including Joseph Stalin at the 1943 Teheran Conference. Stalin found it "cold on the stomach," but apparently liked it.[23]

In 1971, with a thick snow battering the nation's capital, the normally cantankerous Richard Nixon surprised members of the press corps on New Year's Eve by inviting them to the White House for cocktails and conversation while mixing up what he described as his "special formula Martini."

"If he is a connoisseur of anything," a Nixon observer told a reporter from *Saturday Review* in 1969, "it is the martini . . . He is very particular about the brand of gin—he prefers Beefeater—and the way it's mixed . . . Nixon favored the 'In and Out' martini mixed by his friend Bebe Rebozzo in which the vermouth was put into a shaker, swung around once and then thrown away before adding the gin. 'That's very good. Bebe, Very good,' he would say as part of the ritual."[24]

Lyndon Johnson liked the in-and-out martini—a glass filled with vermouth, then dumped out and filled with gin.

 # RUM MARTINI

This drink, also known as the Jean Harlow, was favored by the film actress.

> 2 ounces light rum
> 2 ounces sweet vermouth
> Garnish: lemon peel

PREPARATION Pour the ingredients into a cocktail shaker with ice cubes. Shake well. Strain into a chilled cocktail glass. Garnish with the lemon peel.[25]

MARY PICKFORD

This cocktail was created in Havana by British barman Fred Kaufman, who worked at the Hotel Sevilla, then called the Sevilla-Biltmore Hotel. Pickford was on the island in the early 1920s with her husband Douglas Fairbanks. The cocktail's discovery was cited in the book *When It's Cocktail Time in Cuba* (1928) by Basil Woon.

> 2 ounces white rum
>
> 1 ounce pineapple juice
>
> 1 barspoon grenadine
>
> 1 barspoon Maraschino liqueur
>
> Garnish: brandied cherry

PREPARATION Combine all ingredients and shake with ice. Strain into a chilled glass and garnish.

CULTURAL CONTEXT The drink has remarkable staying power. In October 2013, it was featured on Rachel Maddow's *Cocktail Moment*, a Friday feature on her CNBC show.

MIMOSA

Created in 1925 at the Ritz Hotel in Paris, it was named after a tropical flowering shrub. As Salvatore Calabrese described it in *Classic Cocktails*: "The combination of champagne and orange juice and Grand Marnier produces a similar colour to the Mimosa's sensitive yellow blooms."

> 4 ounces champagne
> ½ ounce Cointreau or Grand Marnier
> 1½ ounces orange juice

PREPARATION Pour the liquor and juice in the bottom of a chilled champagne flute; top up with the champagne slowly so as to not spill the wine from excess carbonation. It is optional to garnish with an orange slice or zest.

MINT JULEP

A long drink consisting of bourbon or rye whiskey, crushed ice, sugar, and fresh mint, mixed together usually following a prescribed procedure on the treatment of the mint leaves. The drink is chiefly associated with the American South, with a strong modern association with the Kentucky Derby. This long-established drink—which was never really out of fashion—reestablished itself during Prohibition, perhaps for nothing more than the simple reason that the strong flavor and smell of fresh mint mitigated the effect of less-than-prime whiskey. The author Irvin S. Cobb's (see *Fish House Rum Punch*) fictional character Old Judge Priest, who appears in *Irvin S. Cobb's Own Recipe Book*, offered this recipe dating back to 1934. Cobb was a bourbon fundamentalist when it came to his juleps and once said of his friend H. L. Mencken: "Any guy who'd put rye in a mint julep and crush the leaves would put scorpions in a baby's bed."[26]

Old Judge Priest Mint Julep . . .

Take from the cold spring some water, pure as angels are; mix it with sugar till it seems like oil. Then take a glass and crush your mint within it with a spoon—crush it around the borders of the glass and leave no place untouched. Then throw the mint away—it is a sacrifice. Fill with cracked ice the glass; pour in the quantity of Bourbon which you want. It trickles slowly through the ice. Let it have time to cool, then pour your sugared water over it. No spoon is needed; no stirring allowed— just let it stand a moment. Then around the brim place sprigs of mint, so that the one who drinks may find taste and odor at one draft.

CULTURAL CONTEXT The first writer to mention the drink was Washington Irving in his *History of New York*, in which he characterized the natives of Lord Baltimore's Maryland ("Merryland," in this context) as people who "were notoriously prone to get fuddled and make merry with mint-julep and apple-toddy." The drink has long been associated with hyperbole and tall tales, as this early 1839 observation attributed to novelist Captain Frederick Marryat illustrates: "They say that you may always know the grave of a Virginian as, from the quantity of julep he has drunk, mint invariably springs up where he has been buried."

§ MOCK CHAMPAGNE

A drink created for the 1930 book *Prohibition Punches*, featuring legal beverages. This one was created by Mrs. Imogene Oakley of Philadelphia, who insisted: "This recipe has all the good qualities of champagne and none of the bad ones."

⅓ white grape juice
⅔ White Rock (club soda)

PREPARATION "The mixture may be half and half if preferred, but too much grape juice diminishes the sparkle of the effervescent water," according to Mrs. Oakley. Serve in long-stemmed champagne glass.

CULTURAL CONTEXT There was a great rush

to create cocktail and punchbowl stand-ins for drinks containing alcohol. First Lady Lou (Mrs. Herbert) Hoover was a fan of punch made with plain spring water (either mineral or charged) and then sweetened and flavored with fruit juice, principally oranges, lemons, grapefruit, and berries of all sorts, but sometimes mixed in the juice of tangerines and kumquats.[27]

THE MONKEY GLAND

A Prohibition classic, the Monkey Gland was devised at Harry's New York Bar in Paris in 1923. The name is a reference to a surgical procedure by a Dr. Serge Voronoff. For men with performance issues, Dr. Voronoff offered to implant in them the testicle of a monkey, for "rejuvenation."

> 1½ ounces gin
> 1½ ounces fresh orange juice
> 1 teaspoon grenadine
> 1 teaspoon absinthe

PREPARATION Pour ingredients into a cocktail shaker and fill with ice. Shake well for 10 seconds and strain into a chilled cocktail glass.

CULTURAL CONTEXT This drink made headlines such as this one from *The Washington Post* of April 29, 1923: NEW COCKTAIL IN PARIS IS THE MONKEY GLAND, which was followed by text that actually gave instructions as to how to prepare one: "For the benefit of friends over in America who have not exhausted their cellars, here is the recipe: half and half gin and orange juice, a dash of absinthe, and a dash of raspberry or other sweet juice. Mix well with ice and serve only with a doctor handy. Inside half an hour the other day Frank purveyed forty of these, to the exclusion of Manhattans and Martinis." *The Post* added: "The monkey gland requires absinthe to be perfect, but its amateurs have found anise a substitute with a sufficient kick."

CAVEAT Cocktail critic Doug Ford has made, tasted, and reviewed the drink on his Cold Glass website and concludes: "It's a good cocktail—in fact, it's a delicious cocktail—but I'm trying to picture myself ordering one across a bar. 'Good evening, Miss, I'll have a Monkey Gland, please. And keep them coming.'"

NEGRONI

According to cocktail historian Gary Regan, this concoction's origins are documented in the book *Sulle Tracce del Conte: La Vera Storia del Cocktail Negroni*, which was written by Lucca Picchi, head bartender at Caffe Rivoire in Florence, Italy. The drink was created at Bar Casoni in Florence, according to Picchi, when Count Camillo Negroni ordered an Americano—sweet vermouth, Campari and club soda—with gin swapped in for the standard soda.

> 1 ounce gin
>
> 1 ounce Campari
>
> ¾ ounce sweet Italian vermouth
>
> Thin slice of orange

PREPARATION Pour the liquids over ice in a rocks glass. Stir and sip.

CULTURAL CONTEXT In a June 2010 article in *Playboy* on classic drinks, A. J. Baime advised: "The Negroni is easy to make at home, but for the ultimate experience, venture to the cafe where it was invented. Though it's now called Caffe Giacosa, it's still in the same place on Via della Spada in Firenze."

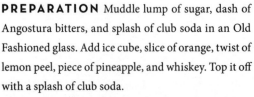

O

OLD FASHIONED

Likely one of the earliest North American cocktails, with the first reference appearing in 1806—this may be one of the oldest of all American drinks, or at least the first for which there is a record. Franklin D. Roosevelt, the President who presided over the end of Prohibition, fa-vored this drink along with his famous Dirty Martini. According Oscar Getz in his book *Whiskey: An American Pictorial History*, this was FDR's preferred formula:

> 1 sugar cube
> 1 dash Angostura bitters
> Club soda
> 2 ounces rye whisky
> Slice of orange
> Twist of lemon peel
> Piece of pineapple

PREPARATION Muddle lump of sugar, dash of Angostura bitters, and splash of club soda in an Old Fashioned glass. Add ice cube, slice of orange, twist of lemon peel, piece of pineapple, and whiskey. Top it off with a splash of club soda.

CULTURAL CONTEXT The Old Fashioned was also the drink preferred by President Harry Truman. He and First Lady Bess each enjoyed one before dinner during their White House years. Truman did not add fruit to his Old Fashioneds, following the advice of Crosby Gaige, who wrote in his 1941 *Cocktail Guide*: "Serious-minded persons omit fruit salad from Old Fashioneds while the frivolous window-dress the brew with slices of orange, sticks of pineapple, and a couple of turnips." The Old Fashioned, which went out of style in the last quarter of the twentieth century, has been given a reprieve as the drink of choice for the character Don Draper on the *Mad Men* cable television series.

ORANGE BLOSSOM

During Prohibition, this was one of the most popular illicit drinks. It is said to have been created in an attempt to mask the taste and odor of "bathtub gin." It is essentially just a mixture of orange juice and gin, although there are many variations using a wide variety of ingredients. *The Old Waldorf Astoria Bar Book* has a recipe for Orange Blossom No. 1:

> ¾ ounce gin
>
> ¾ ounce sweet vermouth (i.e., Cinzano Bianco)
>
> ¾ ounce orange juice

PREPARATION Pour the ingredients into a mixing pitcher or glass filled with ice cubes, stir well, and strain.

CULTURAL CONTEXT One evening in the early 1920s, humorist Robert Benchley stood at the bar at Tony's Restaurant, a popular 49th Street eatery and speakeasy, and turned to his good friend and fellow member of the Algonquin Round Table, Dorothy Parker, and said:

"Let's find out what all the fuss is about."

He then stunned his friends by downing an Orange Blossom cocktail. Although Benchley had frequented the midtown speakeasy scene with his colleagues from *Vanity Fair* and the *New York World*, he had to this point avoided alcohol. While his friends indulged themselves with round after round of bootleg liquor, Benchley had consumed only juice and soft drinks. Now at age thirty-one, he had consumed his first drink. There are other versions of the story that are spelled out in Michael A. Lerner's book *Dry Manhattan: Prohibition in New York City*. But as Lerner then points out: "The exact facts of the story, however, matter much less than what they illustrate. Regardless of when and where Robert Benchley took his first drink, until Prohibition came along he had, in spite of the company he kept, embodied the traditional middle-class Protestant dry. Something about the dry experiment changed Benchley's attitude toward alcohol. He became emblematic of a cultural rebellion against Prohibition that rejected the dry crusade's moral vision for America."*[28]

---

* During Prohibition, the Algonquin Hotel was Dry, which

PARADISE COCKTAIL

The Paradise Cocktail is an example of a drink that got a boost through a cameo appearance in a movie produced during Prohibition. It was Kay Francis and William Powell's drink of choice in *One Way Passage* (1932).

> 1 ounce apricot-flavored brandy
>
> ¾ ounce gin
>
> Juice of ¼ orange

PREPARATION Shake with ice and strain into cocktail glass.

---

applied to the Round Table where civility and sobriety reigned. The members of the group met for drinks after work in Midtown speakeasies. This has not stopped modern writers from assuming that these fabled lunches were boozy—e.g., in Virginia Reynolds's *The Little Black Book of Cocktails: The Essential Guide to New and Old Classics*, the Algonquin is listed and discussed as one of a few "Resplendent Drinking Establishments of Literary Fame."

PARISIAN POUSSE-CAFÉ

This was Marlene Dietrich's entry in the Carmel-by-the-Sea contest, which she described as "very pretty and very tasty."

> ⅖ Curaçao
> ⅖ Kirschwasser
> ⅕ Chartreuse

PREPARATION Use a wineglass that is wet. Pour in the Curaçao; on top of this, the Kirschwasser; and on top of that, the Chartreuse. The dampness of the wineglass will cause each layer—the red, amber, and yellow-green—to lie, sandwich-like, on top of the one below.

CULTURAL CONTEXT A 1966 Broadway musical named *Pousse Café* with music by Duke Ellington was a complete disaster.

§ PRAIRIE OYSTER

A pick-me-up/hangover remedy that appears in *The Speakeasies of 1932* as an offering from John, the bartender at the Log Cabin, a speakeasy in the Fifties east of Seventh Avenue above a garage.

> **2 teaspoons of Worcestershire sauce**
> **Yolk of a fresh egg**
> **Dash of red pepper**
> **Pinch of salt**
> **2 tablespoons of malt vinegar**

PREPARATION Put the Worcestershire sauce in a wineglass. Add the unbroken egg yolk and sprinkle with a little red pepper and salt. Put the malt vinegar on top.

CULTURAL CONTEXT Not to be confused with the original prairie oyster, a testis of a bull calf used as food.

§ PUSSYFOOT

Named after William E. "Pussyfoot" Johnson (1862–1945), a staunch Prohibitionist and respected chief law enforcement officer for the U.S. Indian Service. Johnson implemented effective "catlike policies in pursuing lawbreakers in the Indian Territory," as he himself explained in *Who's Who in America*, obtaining some 4,400 convictions during his tenure (1908–1911). As Albert Marckwardt points out in *American English*: "Johnson was also active in the Anti-Saloon League and frequently lectured on temperance. Not only was he instrumental in the passage of Prohibition in 1919, he took the 'cause' to London, where it was not always met with enthusiasm. In fact at Essex Hall an angry lush in the crowd he was lecturing to threw a stone and blinded him in one eye."

1 ounce lemon juice

2 ounces lime juice

6 ounces orange juice

1 egg yolk

6 ounces cold sparkling water

Garnish: orange slice

PREPARATION Combine lemon, lime, and orange juices, and egg yolk in a cocktail shaker with ice. Shake vigorously and strain into a chilled Tom Collins glass. Top off with the sparkling water. Stir gently. Garnish with orange slice.

ROB ROY

Then as now, the Rob Roy is probably the most famous Scotch-based cocktail. A first cousin to the Manhattan, it was invented in 1897.

½ part Scotch

½ part sweet vermouth

Dash of Angostura Bitters

PREPARATION Shake with cracked ice and strain into a cocktail glass.

CULTURAL CONTEXT Rob Roy was a real historical character, but the name of the drink is a reference to a popular operetta. Opening in New York in October 1894, the hit play's name of Rob Roy served as inspiration for the cocktail because of the reddish color and use of Scotch.

ROCK AND RYE

The Rock and Rye cocktail managed to make its way through Prohibition as both a sweet libation and as a home remedy, often being prescribed medicinally, especially as a cough medicine. The best-known method of preparation was similar to Harry Craddock's, from his 1930 *Savoy Cocktail Book*, which simply called for dosing whiskey with rock candy and lemon.

> 1 teaspoon rock candy syrup or grenadine
> Juice of ½ lemon
> 1 glass rye whiskey

PREPARATION Stir together in the same glass and squeeze lemon peel on top.

CULTURAL CONTEXT In *The Speakeasies of 1932*, there was an establishment called the Dixie, which was hidden behind the false front of a cigar store in the Forties block west of Sixth Avenue. This is the formula for the drink advocated by John the bartender, whom Al Hirschfeld describes as "the kind of man you'd not hesitate to have your mother meet."

ROYAL FIZZ

Bill the bartender at the Stonewall, a speakeasy at 91 Seventh Avenue, suggested this as his libation of choice in *The Speakeasies of 1932*.

> 1 glass gin
> Yolk of fresh egg
> 1 teaspoon grenadine
> Juice of ½ lemon
> Soda water

PREPARATION Shake ingredients well and strain into medium-size tumbler and fill the balance of the glass with soda.

SAZERAC

Purportedly "America's first cocktail," Sazerac is the emblematic drink of New Orleans. Born on a steamy New Orleans street called Rue Royal in 1838, it was the creation of a descendant of an escaped slave named Antoine Peychaud, who assembled a mix of ingredients to make a cocktail that would, as one writer put it, "outlast fads, floods, and whatever else his town could dish out." The original elixir was a combination of cognac, from Sazerac de Forge et Fils in France, and bitters made by Peychaud himself. In 1873, the drink was changed when American rye whiskey was substituted for cognac. A dash of absinthe was added by bartender Leon Lamothe, who is now regarded as the Father of the Sazerac. In 1912, absinthe was banned in the United States because of the presence of wormwood (a supposed hallucinogenic), so Peychaud substituted his special bitters in its place.

> 1 jigger (1½ ounces) rye whiskey
>
> 2 dashes anisette
>
> Dash of Pernod
>
> Dash of Angostura bitters

PREPARATION Shake with cracked ice and strain into cocktail glass. "For this New Orleans powerhouse, the glass must be thoroughly chilled," advise the editors of *Esquire's Handbook for Hosts*.

CULTURAL CONTEXT President-elect Warren G. Harding and a large company of friends and advisers, including his personal physician, visited the Grunewald Hotel in New Orleans. At the Harding party's first luncheon at the hotel after Harding expressed his desire for a drink, scotch and soda highballs were supplied from owner Theodore Grunewald's private stock. According to Meigs O. Frost, the reporter who was at the luncheon, Harding turned to his host:

"Mr. Grunewald, I was in New Orleans a couple of years ago, very quietly, by myself. Just a United States Senator from Ohio on vacation. On one of your streets, Royal Street, I think, I drank a cocktail with an odd name I have forgotten, but a flavor I never forgot. It was the finest cocktail I ever had in my life."

"Was it a Sazerac, Mr. President?" asked Grunewald.

"That's it," said Harding.

"Mr. President," said Grunewald, "this hotel is my personal residence. I stocked my personal cellar before Prohibition became effective. I have all the ingredients, and one of the old Sazerac bartenders works for me here as a waiter in this hotel. Would you care to taste a Sazerac again?"

"I certainly would," Harding replied.

Grunewald stepped to a house phone and gave his

order quietly. Fifteen minutes later, a waiter arrived bearing a huge silver tray laden with Sazeracs in old-fashioned bar glasses.

Harding took a sip, and Frost reported that "a slow smile spread across his face."

He then called across the room to the rest of his party. "Put down those highballs. Come here and taste this! Here's a real drink!"

Grunewald then told Harding, who was about to embark on a cruise leaving from New Orleans, that there would be two bon voyage baskets awaiting Harding in his cabin, and underneath the fruit would be six quarts of Sazeracs. Harding then embraced Grunewald and invited him to stay in the White House during the upcoming Inauguration.[29]

SCOFFLAW

"Scofflaw" was the winning entry in a 1924 competition of the *Boston Herald* that asked readers to coin a new word for those who refused to have their drinking habits dictated by politicians. The word officially made it into the language on January 15, 1924, when the winning entry was announced. Within two weeks of the contest result, the Scofflaw cocktail appeared at Harry's American Bar at 5 Rue Daunou, Paris.[30]

> 1½ ounces rye whiskey
>
> 1 ounce dry vermouth
>
> ¾ ounce fresh lemon juice
>
> ¾ ounce grenadine
>
> Garnish: lemon twist

PREPARATION Combine all ingredients with ice and shake. Strain into a chilled glass and garnish.

CULTURAL CONTEXT The Scofflaw still appears in many cocktail manuals and is a staple of today's speakeasy-style bars. In 2007, Christopher Hirst of *The Independent* (London) revived some drinks of the past for a series on cocktails and raved about the Scofflaw: "Though you might expect a drink concocted in such circumstances to be an unremarkable novelty, the Scofflaw is sensationally good. Ruby red in color, it has an intriguing complexity and an exquisite sweet-sour balance."

SIDECAR

A stiff drink made of cognac, Cointreau, and lemon juice, in a 3–2–1 ratio that's shaken and served up. Created by Harry at Harry's New York Bar, Paris, after the First World War, for an eccentric captain who turned up in a chauffeur-driven motorbike sidecar. It was an immensely popular drink during Prohibition.

¾ ounce Cointreau

¾ ounce lemon juice

1½ ounces cognac

PREPARATION Shake well with cracked ice, then strain into a chilled cocktail glass that has had its outside rim rubbed with lemon juice and dipped in sugar. Serve in a cocktail glass.

CAVEAT Listen to David Wondrich of *Esquire* magazine on this one: "This is a drink whose *suavité* is beyond question—it's the Warren Beatty of modern mixology. It's so easy, in fact, to be seduced by this clever old roué that a word of caution would not be out of place here. These gents have a way of stealing up on you and—bimmo! Next thing you know it's 8:43 on Monday morning and you're sitting in the backseat of a taxi idling in front of your place of employ. In your skivvies."

STUBBY COLLINS

A short Tom Collins popular during the era when short went long (highballs), and long went short.

> 1 ounce lemon juice
>
> 1 teaspoonful fine granulated sugar
>
> 2 ounces dry gin

PREPARATION This drink is served in an Old Fashioned glass. The sugar and lemon juice should be stirred well; then add 2 cubes of crystal clear ice and pour the dry gin over it. Serve with short glass stir rod.

Stubby Collins (Angostura)

Make the same as a Stubby Collins, but add several hearty dashes of Angostura Bitters so as to give it a nice, rich pink color and added zest. This variation appears in *The Professional Mixing Guide or How to Get Drunk Fast*.

TWELVE MILE LIMIT

One of a group of cocktails with names that allude to aspects of the Eighteenth Amendment, the Volstead Act, and the cluster of ancillary legislation that arose around them. *Saveur* magazine, which recently featured the drink, said of it: "The very drink it inspired taunts the measure with its especially strong yet beachy combination of rum, whiskey, brandy, grenadine, and lemon juice."

> 1 ounce silver rum
>
> ½ ounce rye whiskey
>
> ½ ounce brandy
>
> ½ ounce grenadine
>
> ½ ounce fresh lemon juice
>
> Garnish: 1 lemon twist

PREPARATION Combine rum, whiskey, brandy, grenadine, and juice in a cocktail shaker filled with ice; cover and shake until chilled, about 15 seconds. Strain into a chilled highball glass and top with lemon twist.

CULTURAL CONTEXT Indeed, the "rum fleet" itself was a curious flotilla. A 1923 report on Prohibition described some of its elements: "A former Spanish cruiser, once pride of the fleets of the haughty Dons, has been spotted among them. The one-time palatial yacht of a noted American industrial captain has flashed her dainty heels back and forth in the new brotherhood of the coast, keeping company with blunt-nosed and weather-beaten old fishing schooners from the Grand Banks. Smaller craft, made glorious in the war through the daring of Yankee tars who manned them, have joined this pack of sea vermin preying on the self-respect and decency of a people."[31]

W

WARD EIGHT

One of the most popular of all Prohibition cocktails, it came out of the Dry Years a champion—in 1934, *Esquire* magazine named it the drink of the year.

> 2 ounces rye or bourbon whiskey
>
> ¾ ounce freshly squeezed lemon juice
>
> ¾ ounce freshly squeezed orange juice
>
> 1 teaspoon grenadine
>
> Garnish: orange slice and/or Maraschino cherry (optional)

PREPARATION Combine whiskey, lemon juice, orange juice, and grenadine in a cocktail shaker that is half filled with ice. Shake well for at least 30 seconds. Strain mixture into a cocktail glass. Garnish with an orange slice or Maraschino cherry if you wish.

CULTURAL CONTEXT If Boston has a signature drink, it is the Ward Eight. The widely ac-cepted version of its origin was that it was created at Boston's Locke-Ober restaurant in 1898 to celebrate the election victory of Martin Lomasney (aka the Boston Mahatma, aka Czar of Ward 8), who was seeking a seat in the Massachusetts state legislature. Lomasney was the local political machine's power broker in Ward 8 (at Boston's South End). He was famous for saying, "Never write if you can speak; never speak if you can nod; never nod if you can wink."

WHISKEY SOUR

The whiskey sour has a long history in the world of cocktails, making an appearance in the first published cocktail book, Jerry Thomas's 1862 *The Bon Vivant's Companion or How to Mix Drinks*. It has been claimed that the sour evolved from the practice of adding lime juice to rum rations to prevent scurvy among sailors in the British Navy in the 1700s. Although this assertion is hard to prove, it makes sense: fresh fruit was perishable, so the juice would be doctored with rum (or gin, or later sometimes whiskey) in order to preserve the juice as well as to ensure the health of the sailors.

1 large teaspoon powdered white sugar, dissolved in a little seltzer or Apollinaris water

Juice of ½ small lemon

1 wineglass bourbon or rye whiskey

PREPARATION Fill the glass full of shaved ice, shake up, and strain into a claret glass. Ornament with berries.

CULTURAL CONTEXT A columnist writing in the *Charlotte News* (North Carolina) during Prohibition was quoted by Fletcher Dobyns in *The Amazing Story of Repeal* on the subject of bringing women into the speakeasies. It alluded to the palliative use of whiskey sours: "And so it is. I have seen women with snowy hair and wrinkled faces sipping cocktails with 'purty gals' who looked to be still in their teens, and have watched them walk unsteadily from the table after using a few whisky sours and a bottle or so of beer to hold down the cocktails they had imbibed." The columnist added that the Prohibitionists promised to abolish the old saloon "and it has been done. No brass rails here. No longer is the grogshop a man's institution. Under soft lights, to the strains of dreamy music, the boys and 'gals' sit at tables, are waited on by uniformed youngsters, and, oh, well."[32]

YALE COCKTAIL

Cocktails named for colleges and universities date back to the 1890s when they were introduced at the Holland House bar in Manhattan. This one survived as a popular Prohibition drink.

> 1 dash orange bitters
> 1 dash Pernod
> 1½ ounces gin

PREPARATION Shake well with cracked ice, strain, and serve in cocktail glass. Twist of Lemon peel, for oil.

CULTURAL CONTEXT It is right and fitting that this cocktail, which was popular during Prohibition, be included in this collection. Yale and the state of Connecticut were especially loathed by the Drys because of their opposition to Prohibition. "Not only is the Yale student sentiment prevailingly wet," wrote Irving Fisher in his 1926 plea for more stringent enforcement, "but the city and state in which Yale is located are among the wettest in the Nation." Fisher, a Yale economics professor, dwelt on the Yale undergraduate: "Besides living in this damp atmosphere, the students largely come from the great Wet cities, especially New York, and a large fraction of the students are from homes of the well-to-do who can support wine cellars."[34]

GLOSSARY OF VOLSTEAD ENGLISH

One of the great unintended consequences of Prohibition was the vast, slangy impact it had on American English and then, by extension, the English language at large. Prohibition begat *organized crime*—both the institution and the term—and sparked the rebellion and mores that put the roar in the Roaring Twenties, and gave rhythm and syncopation to the Jazz Age, each of which contributed rich lexicons of their own. There were those who would go so far to suggest that the language was *hi-jacked* as gangster slang and that style was emulated in popular culture, a development that was as impossible to stem as was the flow of bootleg booze.

With Repeal it became obvious that Americans were talking differently than they had before the enactment of the Eighteenth Amendment. As noted in the *New York Herald Tribune*, November 8, 1933: "Prohibition enriched the language with many new words, revived long forgotten expressions and made popular countless previously obscure terms and nomenclature."

Lexicons were assembled, often in unlikely places. *The Stone Cutters' Journal* in a 1933 issue published an A-to-Z of *Vocabulary Enriched During Dry Era*, which was introduced with this line: "No great event, not even the World War, gave the

United States a greater abundance of sling words and phrases in the dry era."

Here is a smattering of the words and phrases that came into the language as a result of Prohibition.

ABC A cocktail containing "a little of everything."

age of pain The Volstead era to its detractors.

alcoholiday One of many synonyms for the Prohibition Era.

appetizer One of countless synonyms for a "drink" during Prohibition. In 1926, a magazine devoted to college humor titled *College Inn* carried an A-to-Z list of synonyms "according to the modern undergraduate."

A—APPETIZER	N—Nip
B—BRACER	O—OINTMENT
C—CHUCKLE	P—POISON
D—DIVIDEND	Q—QUICK ONE
E—Eye-Opener	R—Rinse
F—FINGER	S—Slug
G—GARGLE	T—TIPPY
H—HAIR-CURLER	U—UP-AND-DOWN
I—INK	V—VAPOR
J—JOYFUL JUICE	W—WHISTLE-WETTER
K—KICK KIT	X—X-RAY
L—LIFTER	Y—YEAST
M—MERRY-WATER	Z—ZIPPER

bathtub gin Name for small-batch gin during Prohibition that got its name from the fact that grain alcohol, glycerin, and juice of juniper berries were mixed in bottles or jugs too tall to be filled with water from a sink tap so they were commonly filled under a bathtub tap. The term first appeared in 1920 as a direct reference to the poor-quality alcohol that was being made. Though the phrase references gin specifically, it came to be used as a general term for any type of cheap homemade booze. However, because distilling was illegal during Prohibition, denatured alcohol was used when grain alcohol wasn't available, which led to illness, blindness, or death in many cases.

beer baron Mock honorific title for the head of a group manufacturing and distributing the illegal product.

blind pig A place where liquor is illicitly sold. The operator of an establishment (such as a saloon or bar) would charge customers to see an attraction (such as an actual blind farm animal) and then serve a "complimentary" alcoholic beverage, thus circumventing the law. During Prohibition, the difference between a speakeasy and a blind pig was that a speakeasy was usually a higher-class establishment that offered food and, at the highest end of the scale, entertainment. In large cities, some speakeasies even required a coat and tie for men, and evening dress for women. But a blind pig was usually a low-class dive where only beer and liquor were offered. The *Oxford English Dictionary* cites the first appearance as 1887 in a Minnesota statute: "Whoever shall attempt to evade or violate any of the laws of this state by means of the artifice or contrivance known as the 'Blind Pig' or 'Hole in the Wall' shall be punished."[1]

blue ruin Slang term for gin, along with laughing soup, juniper juice, and tittery. Blue ruin later became a term for any human disaster.

bootician High-end bootlegger. A coinage belonging to H. L. Mencken, who wrote: "I proposed the use of bootician to designate a high-toned big-city bootlegger in the *American Mercury*, April 1925. The term met a crying need, and had considerable success. In March 1927, the *San Jose Mercury-Herald* said: 'Our bootleggers are now calling themselves booticians. It seems that bootlegger has some trace of odium about it, while bootician has none.'" Mencken was also alleged to have invented the term "boozehound."

bootleg Describing alcohol—or any other product—that is made or sold illegally. Etymologist Michael Quinion terms it a surprisingly late coinage, first being recorded from Omaha, Nebraska in 1889 (with the related bootlegger being recorded in Oklahoma the same year). Prohibition gave it a huge boost, of course. Bootleg was at first a literal term. In the days when horsemen wore long boots, their bootlegs were good places to keep objects out of sight. For example, this description comes from *The War in Kansas* by G. Douglas Brewerton of 1856: "He sports

a sky-blue blanket overcoat (a favorite color in Missouri), from the side-pocket of which the butt of a six-shooter peeps threateningly out, and if you will take a look into his right bootleg, we should say that a serviceable bowie-knife might be found inserted between the leather and his tucked-in Kentucky jean pantaloons."

bootlegger An individual who illegally makes, transports, or sells alcoholic beverages.

bootlegging Illegally producing, transporting, or selling alcoholic

A woman in Washington, D.C., reveals a flask in her boot.

beverages. Al Capone attempted to put the term in context: "When I sell liquor, it's called bootlegging; when my patrons serve it on Lake Shore Drive, its called hospitality."

booze cruise A voyage on which passengers were taken just far enough from the shoreline to be outside U.S. jurisdiction, so that they could buy and consume alcohol legally. Also known as a *whoopee cruise.*

bricks of wine Dehydrated compressed blocks or "bricks" of wine were widely sold during Prohibition because it was not illegal to produce wine at home for personal consumption. The bricks were reconstituted with water and used to make wine. The bricks came with a label that read:

> WARNING: After dissolving the brick in a gallon of water, do not place the liquid in a jug away in the cupboard for twenty days because then it would turn into wine.

Bronx Cheer Slang for the Bronx cocktail, also known as the Razzberry—a play on the sound of contempt made by vibrating the tongue between the lips.

Bureau of Prohibition The Federal agency established to enforce National Prohibition. It was characterized by rampant corruption and public disdain.

burlock A special rum-runner package containing six straw-jacketed bottles, three on the bottom layer, two in the middle, and one on top. The bottles were sewed tightly in burlap. Liquor packed in burlocks required a third less space in the hold of a vessel than when shipped in the ordinary bulky, wooden boxes. Rumrunner McCoy is generally credited with the invention of the "burlock," which revolutionized methods of loading and stowing liquor cargoes.[2]

butter and egg man The money man, the man with the bankroll, a yokel who comes to town to blow a big wad in nightclubs; a free spender. "Look who just walked in—a big butter and egg man from Fort Wayne."

chef The person in charge of an alcohol distilling plant.

Chicago lightning Gunfire. With the rise of Al Capone and his gang wars and especially in the wake of the 1929 St. Valentine's Day Massacre; the noun *Chicago* became a synonym for *violence*. Vis:

Chicago overcoat Coffin.

Chicago piano / Chicago typewriter Machine gun, specifically the Thompson submachine gun or Tommy gun.

clip joint A place of entertainment in which customers are tricked into paying highly inflated prices for inferior goods or services, or even none at all, and then coerced into paying.

corn liquor Alcoholic beverage distilled from corn mash that varied in potability from acceptable to godawful. Just after Repeal, humorist Irvin S. Cobb offered this description: "It smells like gangrene starting in a mildewed silo; it tastes like the wrath to come, and when you absorb a deep swig of it you have all the sensations of having swallowed a lighted kerosene lamp. A sudden violent jolt of it has been known to stop the victim's watch, snap both his suspenders and crack his glass eye right across—all in the same motion."[3]

cut Describing liquor that has been adulterated, especially imported Scotch that has been diluted.

do re mi Money.

drugstore During Prohibition, places that sold booze by the bottle were known as "drugstores"—a euphemism which is lost on modern readers of F. Scott Fitzgerald's *The Great Gatsby*:

> "I found out what your 'drug-stores' were." He turned to us and spoke rapidly. "He and this Wolfsheim bought up a lot of side-street drug-stores here and in Chicago and sold grain alcohol over the counter. That's one of his little stunts. I picked him for a bootlegger the first time I saw him, and I wasn't far wrong."

Dry A person who supported Prohibition, and a dry area is one in which the purchase of alcoholic beverage is legally prohibited. During Prohibition, it was common to see this term capitalized, as was the antonym *Wet*. As Chas Hardin wrote in *American Speech* in 1931: "There are all the degrees of dryness: *medium dryish, optimistically dry, cracker dry, bone-dry, ultra-dry, fanatical dry,* and *most arid*." Hardin added: "The term *dry* has been used as an adjective, noun, and verb, as in: "I hope to goodness Hoover *dries* the country up." Under a picture

Politicians in support of going "bone dry." William D. Upshaw at right. Photograph taken in D.C. between 1923–1929.

of Andrew McCampbell, one finds "To Dry Up the Undryable."[14] Under A. W. Woodcock's picture is the title "Dryer-Up." An interesting term referring to the supporter of the Volstead Act is *Drymedaries*, evidently derived from dromedaries.

fire extinguisher Anyone who monitors and controls; a chaperone, a killjoy, an *alarm clock*.

gin mill A rundown or seedy nightclub or bar. An establishment where hard liquor is sold; bar.

gintellectual Term coined by Broadway columnist Walter Winchell for the writers, artists, and others creative types who populated Manhattan speakeasies during the Dry Years.

Hadacol A patent medicine popular during Prohibition that *Time* magazine said had a kick equivalent to a vitamin-enriched Manhattan cocktail.

heist A holdup; robbery or hijacking. It is possibly/probably a corruption of *hoist* (as in *hoist your hands up*). The first citation in the *Oxford English Dictionary* is in 1930 from a book titled *Chicago Surrenders*, suggesting the term may have originated in the Windy City.

hijack To steal another person's liquor at gunpoint. "I would have had $50,000," said Jimmy, "if I hadn't been hijacked." It is the first use of the term cited by the *Oxford English Dictionary* from the August 4, 1923, edition of the *Literary Digest*. The practice was central to the lawlessness of what has been called the lawless decade. As Preston William Slosson wrote in 1930 in *The Great Crusade and After*: "The automobile provided the smuggler with a new facility. Huge trucks, moving by night at high speed along the highways, conveyed millions of gallons of liquor into the United States. The hazards were always great, but the greater the risk the higher were the prices and profits on each delivery.

Besides the risk of encountering the lawful authorities, the rumrunner had to beware a new and lawless enemy, the 'hijacker.' The hijacker was the pirate of the landward trails. He found his richest source of revenue in holding up rumrunners because his victims, themselves outlaws, dared not call in the aid of the law. But bootleggers, not willing to submit to this imposition, often hired professional gunmen to fight or punish the hijackers—a fruitful source of the gang wars in Chicago and elsewhere."[4]

The oft-repeated story is that the term originated as criminals would hold up at gunpoint trucks carrying loads of contraband whiskey with the command "Stick 'em high, Jack!" or that the crooks would pretend to be friends of the bootleggers by calling out, "Hi, Jack!" However, there is no evidence of this origin that has come to light, and the term is listed as of unknown origin in modern dictionaries.

Although the term was first recorded in 1923, but the modern connotation of commandeering a vehicle, especially an aircraft, and the killing or ransoming of its occupants, dates from the 1960s—*skyjack* and *carjack* being extended forms of the word.

The term *jack*—to steal—is, according to the *Oxford English Dictionary*, a backformation of *hijack*.

The Hour The cocktail hour, for short. It came into its own during Prohibition when it became a sacrament to the determined scofflaw. Herbert Hoover once described it as "the pause between the errors and trials of the day and the hopes of the night."

imported Code word for *liquor*. According to an article in *Literary Digest*, patrons would ask for "ginger ale" in restaurants, hoping the server would respond with a wink and the query "Imported or domestic?" "If the customer wanted imported ginger ale, and he is the right kind of customer," the magazine explained, "he gets a regulation pre-Prohibition highball."

jack To steal—hijack, for short.

jake leg A paralysis or loss of muscle control in the hands and feet, due to an overconsumption of Jamaican ginger, aka Jake, a legal substance with an alcoholic base. The numbness led sufferers to walk with a distinct gait that was also known as *jake foot.*

John Barleycorn Personification of the grain used to produce liquor, which became the embodiment of the right to have a legal drink. "Well, here comes old man John Barleycorn, stalking back among us, big as life, standing up in his own lawful boots," is how one magazine spoke of him when Prohibition was repealed.

juice joint An illegal drinking establishment; a speakeasy.

lap Liquor.

legger Bootlegger, for short.

Methodist hellenium *Prohibition* by another name for those Wets who blamed the influence of the Methodists for the Volstead Act. The term may have been coined by H. L. Mencken, who uses the term as a synonym for Prohibition in *The American Language.* At one point in the classic work, he alluded to a Baltimore bartender named Raymond E. Sullivan, "whose great talents I often enjoyed at the Belvedere Hotel in Baltimore before the Methodist hellenium."[5]

mob A gang of violent criminals working together to commit crime. *Oxford English Dictionary* dates the term to 1927. Dashiell Hammett was an early user of the term in his 1929 novel *Red Harvest*: "He was in on the Keystone Trust knock-over in Philly two years ago, when Scissors Haggerty's mob croaked two messengers."

muscle in To force one's way into another's liquor territory.

near beer A malt beverage resembling beer but containing no alcohol or no more than a mandated low percentage of alcohol. During Prohibition, it described a brew that contained no more than one half of 1 percent alcohol, which was deemed so weak that Will Rodgers said, "You have to take a glass of water as a stimulant immediately afterward." Near beer was made by brewing real beer, then boiling off the alcohol to conform to the .05 limit. Not surprisingly, a goodly share of real beer never made it to the de-alcoholizer, either by clever deceit of the brewer or by greed of the crooked Prohibition agent.

needle beer Legal near beer into which alcohol was reintroduced often with the aid of a large syringe.

The New Freedom Repeal.

Noble Experiment Another name for National Prohibition, usually used by supporters and occasionally derisively by opponents. The term was applied to Prohibition and widely attributed to President Herbert Hoover, who denied authorship. Hoover's actual words were: "Our country has deliberately undertaken a great social and economic experiment, noble in motive and far-reaching in purpose."

old pal The cocktail, a term used at the beginning of Prohibition.

omnibibulous A term coined by H. L. Mencken to describe his love of alcohol; he noted: "I'm omnibibulous. I drink every known alcoholic drink and enjoy them all." Mencken avoided all drinks during daylight and claimed to avoid none after dark.

organized crime Describing criminals whose actions are coordinated and who operate under a strict hierarchy. The term may have originated from the title of the 1929 book by J. Landesco called *Organized*

Crime in Chicago, which the *Oxford English Dictionary* lists as the first citation for the term.

The Prohibition Error The Prohibition Era.

Pro-inhibition Blend of *prohibition* and *inhibition*.

rib flask A container for liquor conforming to the shape of the rib cage with a capacity of one to two quarts of liquid.

Rum Fleet A curious flotilla of ships laying offshore to sell liquor. A 1923 report on Prohibition described some of its elements: "A former Spanish cruiser, once pride of the fleets of the haughty Dons, has been spotted among them. The one-time palatial yacht of a noted American industrial captain has flashed her dainty heels back and forth in the new brotherhood of the coast, keeping company with blunt-nosed and weather-beaten old fishing schooners from the Grand Banks. Smaller craft, made glorious in the war through the daring of Yankee tars who manned them, have joined this pack of sea vermin preying on the self-respect and decency of a people."[6]

Rum Row Name given to line of ships that anchored just beyond the three-mile limit from Maine to the Carolinas with New York as the epicenter. The ships carried liquor, and would off-load it onto small speedboats that took it ashore. The maritime limit was three miles prior to April 21, 1924, and twelve miles thereafter.

rummie Rumrunner for short.

rumrunner Person or ship engaged in bringing prohibited liquor ashore or across a border. The term came into being in 1920, according to *Merriam-Webster*.

scofflaw One who drank to spite and in spite of Prohibition. In early

January 1924, it was reported that, in support of the three-year-old national policy of Prohibition, Delcevare King, a prominent member of Boston Republican society and an ardent Dry, would give $200 in gold to the person who invented the best word to denounce a violator of the Eighteenth Amendment: "I do seek a word which will stay awake the conscience of the drinker . . . and stab awake the public conscience to the fact that such lawless drinking is, in the words of President Harding, 'a menace to the republic itself.'"

Along with two other Dry judges, King received more than 20,000 entries. They included *boozshevic, contralaw, klinker, lawjacker, slacklaw,* and *wetocrat*. In the end, two people came up with *scofflaw,* winning $100 apiece in gold—Henry Irving Dale of Andover and Kate L. Butler of Dorchester, who dreamed it up while on a train returning from vacation in New Haven. King described his criteria for the selection: He was looking for a word of no more than one or two syllables; starting with "s" ("such words having a sting"); and applicable to any legal violation.

The very sound of the word *scofflaw* appealed to Americans, who were soon creating nonce words with feeble attempts at humor, such as one that started like this: "The *scofflaw* entered the *scoffsaloon*. He leaned an elbow on the *scoffbar* and rested a foot on the *scoffrail*. 'Waddle'y' have?' said the *scoffbartender*."

setup All that is required for an alcoholic drink except the liquor, as a glass, ice, and soda water or, as was often the case during Prohibition, ginger ale, served to patrons who provide their own liquor. Many establishments continued to operate during Prohibition under the assumption that the serving of "set-ups" was legal. 1929 proved to be the year when federal raids became irrational. Federal agents raided the upscale and law-abiding Central Part Casino, arresting the whole staff on the charge of selling "setups" into which one might pour liquor.

Stanley Walker later wrote of the raid: "Some very nice people were at the Casino and they were angry. Such a raid helped to cheapen the government, and to bring the agents into lower esteem than ever, for at the casino no crime was being committed, no poison was being dispensed, and it certainly was not the sort of place where crooks were gathered to hatch their sinister plots."[7]

snooper Pejorative name for Prohibition agent, which went beyond street slang and into the vocabulary of journalists like Stanley Walker, who wrote in 1933 in *The Night Club Era*: "The speakeasy in the nightclub made New York the heaven of the swinish Prohibition agent. Other towns might have their good points, their lucrative graft and comfortable living, but New York, the West, the wicked and the wealthy, was where all the snoopers hope to go before they died."[8]

speak Short for *speakeasy*, a term first brought to public attention in Damon Runyon's *Guys and Dolls*, in which characters talked about "a little speak around the corner."

speakeasy An illegal drinking establishment that was so called because one typically had to whisper a code word or name through a slot in a locked door to gain admittance. Mencken believes the term came from an old Irish term for drinking place.

spigot-bigot The antonym for *scofflaw* awarded by the *Harvard Advocate* from 3,280 terms entered in a contest. The word's creator was Katherine Greene Welling of New York City who also received a summa cum laude from the literary magazine for the terms *cocktail flea*, *water baby*, *cornhawk*, and *aquadack*. Other high-ranking terms in the contest: *jug-buster*, *smugger*, *cookie-pusher*, and *camelouse*.[9]

strip-and-go-naked Jazz Age slang for *gin*.

teetotaler A person who abstains from the consumption of alcohol. The phrase is believed to have originated within the Prohibition Era's temperance societies, where members would add a "T" to their signatures to indicate total abstinence (T + total-ers).

tin roof A free drink—i.e., one that is on the house.

Volstead Act The popular name for the National Prohibition Act of 1919 that was the enabling legislation making possible the enforcement of the Eighteenth Amendment (Prohibition Amendment). The act carried the name of its sponsor Representative Andrew John

An anti-Prohibitionist, 1923.

Volstead (1860–1947), Chairman of the House Judiciary Committee, who managed its passage. *Pre-Volstead* and *post-Volstead* were commonly used for decades, as was the noun *Volsteadism.* Lexicographer Achsah Hardin even found a verb derivative: "The Turlington Act *out-volsteads* Volstead." The adjective *Volsteadian* was often used during the period and does appear as an entry in *Merriam-Webster.*

Wet Those who approved of alcoholic beverages and opposed Prohibition. Factions and party organizations have been formed for and against Prohibition. As Achsah Hardin reported in *American Speech*: "Qualifying terms for those favoring the repeal of the eighteenth amendment are numerous. *Wet* has varying degrees, beginning with *dampish* and becoming *Wet as the Atlantic Ocean.* Arranging these in order we have *dampish, moist, Wettish, Wetter, pessimistically Wet, soaking Wet, sopping Wet, dripping* and *dripping Wet, Wet enough for rubber boots*, and *Wet as the Atlantic Ocean.*

whoopee To have a good time.

wire tap Name given to a new procedure used by the Federal government to trap bootleggers and rumrunners. The first man convicted who appealed claiming the tap was unconstitutional was Roy Olmstead, a former Seattle police officer, who became known as the "king of the bootleggers" of Puget Sound. Olmstead ran a fleet of ships that carried liquor from Canada to islands in the Sound, where speedboats were loaded to whisk the contraband to waiting trucks and cars owned by Olmstead. By 1925, this enterprise was earning $2 million a year, making it a major target for agents of the Department of Justice's Bureau of Investigation.* Olmstead's phones were tapped, and records of the taps

---

* The Bureau of Investigation, headed by young J. Edgar Hoover, became the Federal Bureau of Investigation (FBI) in 1935.

were used as evidence to convict Olmstead and twenty others in 1926. Olmstead, sentenced to four years in prison and fined $8,000, appealed, saying that obtaining evidence by wiretaps was unconstitutional. He argued that his right to privacy and against self-incrimination, under the Fourth and Fifth Amendments, had been violated.[10] The Supreme Court disagreed, ruling by a 5–4 majority that the taps did not violate the Constitution. (Justice Louis Brandeis dissented, saying that the invasion of privacy by wiretapping was even worse than tampering with the mails. "Whenever a telephone line is tapped," he wrote, "the privacy of the persons at both ends of the line is invaded, and all conversations between them upon any subject . . . may be overheard. Moreover, the tapping of one man's telephone line involves the tapping of the telephone of every other person whom he may call, or who may call him. As a means of espionage, writs of assistance and general warrants are but puny instruments of tyranny and oppression when compared with wire tapping.")[11]

ANNOTATED BIBLIOGRAPHY

Ade, George. *The Old Time Saloon—Not Wet—Not Dry Just History*, New York. Ray Long & Richard R. Smith, Inc. 1931.

"All mixed up; the problem with most bartenders these days? They don't know how to make drinks. A toast to some of today's greatest cocktails, as they were originally mixed by the masters themselves." *Playboy*, May 2004: 83.

American Cocktail: 50 Recipes That Celebrate the Craft of Mixing Drinks from Coast to Coast. San Francisco: Chronicle Books, 2011.

Arthur, Stanley Clisby. *Famous New Orleans Drinks And How to Mix 'em.* New Orleans: Harmanson, 1937.

Baime, A. J. "Old School: A Study in the Classics." *Playboy*, June 2010.

Baker, Charles. *The Gentleman's Companion.* 1939. Published initially in two volumes. The first edition is relatively easy to find, but expensive. Volume I pertains to food. Volume II pertains to cocktails. Both volumes are in print as separate books.

Barnes, Bart. "Roger Butts Dies at 89; Arrested Bootleggers on Hill." *Washington Post.* December 12, 1998, p. M-1.

Behr, Edward. *Prohibition: Thirteen Years That Changed America.* Reprint ed. New York: Arcade Publishing, 2011.

Blumenthal, Karen. *Bootleg: Murder, Moonshine, and the Lawless Years of Prohibition.* Reprint ed. publication place: Square Fish, 2013.

Bobrow, Warren. *Apothecary Cocktails: Restorative Drinks from Yesterday and Today.* Beverly, Massachusetts: Fair Winds Press, 2013.

Burnham, John C., ed. *Bad Habits: Drinking, Smoking, Taking Drugs, Gambling, Sexual Misbehavior and Swearing in American History* (American Social Experience). New York: NYU Press, 1994.

Burns, Eric. *The Spirits of America: A Social History of Alcohol.* Philadelphia, Pa.: Temple University Press, 2004.

Calabrese, Salvatore. *Classic Cocktails.* New York, Main Street, 2006.

Calloway, Cab, and Bryant Rollins. *Of Minnie the Moocher and Me.* Edited by John Shearer. New York: Thomas Y. Crowell Company, 1976.

Cerwin, Herbert, and Jo J. Mora. *Cocktail Recipes Mixed By Famous People For A Famous Hotel,* 1933. (These recipes were collected from all parts of the country by The National Association for Advancement of Fine Art of Drinking in the year that brought the end of the long drought 1933. They were tested and sampled by a group of competent experts at Hotel Del Monte. Contributors to this unique collection of mixed drinks include Ernest Hemingway, Theodore Dreiser, Edgar Rice Burroughs, the Marx Brothers, Marlene Dietrich, Will Sparks, George M. Cohan, Ed Wynn, W. C. Fields, and Jo Mora. A faithful reproduction of the scarce 1933 Edition was reprinted in 2004 by the Pebble Beach Company under the title Cocktail Recipes for a Famous Hotel.)

Cipriani, Arrigo. *Harry's Bar: The Life and Times of the Legendary Venice Landmark.* New York: Arcade Publishing, 1996.

Clark, Norman H. *Deliver Us from Evil: An Interpretation of American Prohibition.* The Norton Essays in American History. New York: Norton, 1976.

Cobb, Irvin S. *Irvin S. Cobb's own Recipe Book, The Greatest Drinking Guide ever Published.* Louisville, Kentucky: Frankfort Distilleries, 1934.

Collins, Philip. *Classic Cocktails of the Prohibition Era: 100 Classic Cocktail Recipes.* Los Angeles: General Pub. Group, 1997.

Conrad, Barnaby, III. *The Martini.* San Francisco: Chronicle Books, 1995.

Craddock, Harry. *The Savoy Cocktail Book. Being in the main a complete compendium of the Cocktails, Rickeys, Daisies, Slings, Shrubs, Smashes, Fizzes, Juleps, Cobblers, Fixes, and other Drinks, known and vastly appreciated in this year of grace 1930, with sundry notes of amusement and interest con-*

cerning them, together with subtle Observations upon Wine and their special occasions. Being in the particular an elucidation of the Manners and Customs of people of quality in a period of some equality.

Crockett, Albert Stevens. *Old Waldorf Bar Days; With The Cognomina And Composition Of Four Hundred And Ninety-One Appealing Appetizers And Salutary Potations Long Known, Admired And Served At The Famous Big Brass Rail; Also, A Glossary For The Use Of Antiquarians And Students Of American Mores.* New York: Aventine Press, 1931.

Davis, Marni. *Jews and Booze: Becoming American in the Age of Prohibition.* New York: New York University Press, 2012.

DeGroff, Dale. *The Essential Cocktail: The Art of Mixing Perfect Drinks.* New York: Clarkson Potter/Publishers. 2008.

DeVoto, Bernard. *The Hour.* Portland, Oregon.: Tin House Books, 2010.

Dobyns, Fletcher. *The Story of Repeal; an exposé of the power of propaganda.* Chicago: Willett, Clark & Company, 1940.

Duffy, Patrick Gavin. *Official Mixer's Manual.* 1934.

—. *The Standard Bartender's Guide.* 1934, 1940, 1948 editions.

Edmunds, Lowell. *Martini, Straight Up: The Classic American Cocktail.* Rev. ed. Baltimore: Johns Hopkins University Press, 1998.

—. *The Silver Bullet: The Martini in American Civilization.* Westport, CT: Greenwood Press, 1981.

Embury, David. *The Fine Art of Mixing Drinks.* 1948 (reprinted recently by Mud Puddle Books, Inc., New York).

Felten, Eric. *How's Your Drink? Cocktails, Culture, and the Art of Drinking Well.* Chicago: Agate Surrey, 2009.

Field, Colin Peter. *The Cocktails of The Ritz Paris.* New York: Simon & Schuster. 2003.

Fisher, Irving. *Prohibition at Its Worst.* New York: Macmillan, 1926. He is Professor of Economics, Yale University.

Fitzpatrick, Kevin C. *Under the Table: a Dorothy Parker Cocktail Guide.* Guilford, CT: Lyons Press, 2013.

Fougner, G. Selmer. *Along the Wine Trail: an Anthology of Wines And Spirits.* Boston: The Stratford Company, 1935 (The Sun Printing and Publishing Association, 1934).

Gaige, Crosby. *Crosby Gaige's Cocktail Guide and Ladies' Companion*. Richly Embellished with Drawings Almost from Life by Rea Irvin. With a Foreword in Golden Prose by Lucius Beebe and a Recessional or Final Insult Hurled at the Reader by Lawton Mackall, Published for Hussies and Homebodies by M. Barrows and Company, New York, 1941.

Getz, Oscar. *Whiskey: An American Pictorial History*, with the collaboration of Irv. Bilow. New York, David McKay, 1978.

Grauer, Neil A. "The Speakeasies I Remember: In a Last Conversation before His Death at 99 This January, the Artist Recalled the Places He Visited, Drew, and Wrote about during Prohibition in New York City. You Can Still Lift a Glass at a Couple of Them. (Al Hirschfeld)," *American Heritage*, June–July 2003.

Grimes, William. *Straight up or On the Rocks: A Cultural History of American Drink*. New York: Simon & Schuster, 1993.

Grosset & Dunlap. *Esquire's Handbook for Hosts*. New York: Funk & Wagnalls Company, 1949.

Guyer, William. *The Merry Mixer or Cocktails and Their Ilk: a Booklet On Mixtures and Mulches, Fizzes and Whizzes*. New York: Jos. S. Finch & Co., 1933.

Haimo, Oscar. *Cocktail and Wine Digest, the Barmen's Bible*. New York: Oscar Haimo, 1946.

Hardin, Achsah. Volstead English, American Speech, Vol. VII, Number 2, December 1931.

Hemingway, illustrated by Edward. *Hemingway and Bailey's Bartending Guide to Great American Writers*. Chapel Hill, N.C.: Algonquin Books, 2006.

Hirschfeld, Al. *The Speakeasies of 1932*. Milwaukee, WI: Glenn Young Books, 2003. Originally published on January 1, 1932, under the title *Manhattan Oases; New York's 1932 Speak-Easies* by Dutton. The 2013 reprint has an introduction by Pete Hamill.

Hirst, Christopher. "PICK OF THE MIX; for the Past 101 Weeks on These Pages, Christopher Hirst Has Been Celebrating Great Cocktails. as the Series Reaches Its He Serves Up His Top 10. Illustrations by Lucy Vigrass," *The Independent* (London, England), March 3, 2007.

Jackson, Michael. *Michael Jackson's Bar and Cocktail Companion: The Connois-*

seur's Handbook. Philadelphia: Running Press, 1995; originally published 1979.

Ley, S. Henri.(illustrations by John Held, Jr. The Merry Mixer. New York: Jos. S. Finch & Co., 1935. (The recipes printed in The Merry Mixer include many made famous in the past at such world-renowned New York bars as the old and new Waldorf, the Ritz Carlton, the Old Knickerbocker, Delmonico's, Sherry's, and many other places of equal prominence throughout the United States.)

Mason, Dexter. The Art of Drinking—or What to Make with What You Have (Together with Divers Succulent Canapés Suitable to Each Occasion). New York: Farrar & Rinehart, 1930.

Mencken, H. L. The Vocabulary of the Drinking Chamber, New Yorker, Nov. 6, 1948.

Mills, Eric. Chesapeake Rumrunners of the Roaring Twenties. Centreville, MD. Tidewater Publishers, 2000.

Mitchell, Joseph. Up in the Old Hotel. Revised ed. New York: Vintage, 1993.

Moray, Alastair. The Diary of a Rum-Runner. Boston: Houghton, 1929.

North, Sterling and Carl Kroth. So Red the Nose or Breath in the Afternoon. New York: Farrah and Rinehart, 1935. A compilation of thirty-five cocktail recipes submitted by thirty-five famous authors, such as Ernest Hemmingway's Death in the Afternoon Cocktail, Christopher Morley's Swiss Family Martini, Irving Stone's Lust for Life Cocktail, etc., etc. Each drink is accompanied by an illustration by Roy C. Nelson and a short write up about it and/or the author, done by the author and/or editors. This book commands high prices—several available on line in late 2014 ranging from $200–$800.

Peck, Garrett. Prohibition in Washington, D.C.: How Dry We Weren't. Charleston, SC: History Press, 2011.

Pett, Saul. "Speakeasy Bouncer Remembers Fun and Frolic of the Twenties." Milwaukee Journal, July 18, 1958.

Powers, Richard. Bottoms Up—52 Cock-Tail Spins for High Flyers. Stanford: Redowa Press, 2013. (This is an annotated reprint of one of the rarest of the Prohibition-era cocktail recipe book, die-cut in the shape of a cocktail shaker, was published in the U.S. in 1928, at the height of the Prohibition Era, flaunting the ban on alcohol with cocktail recipes by famous silent film stars, vaudeville performers and musicians, including W. C. Fields, Fanny Brice, Florenz Ziegfield, Ted Lewis and George Gershwin.

Reed, Ben. *Gatsby Cocktails: Classic Cocktails from the Jazz Age*. London: Ryland Peters & Small, 2012.

Regan, Gary. "Shaken and Stirred: When Is a Martini Really a Martini?" *Nation's Restaurant News*, April 14, 1997, 45.

—. *The Joy of Mixology*. New York: Clarkson Potter, 2004.

Reinhardt, Charles Nicholas. *"Cheerio!": a Book of Punches And Cocktails. How to Mix Them, And Other Rare, Exquisite And Delicate Drinks*. 1930.

Reynolds, Virginia. *The Little Black Book of Cocktails: the Essential Guide to New and Old Classics*. White Plains, NY: Peter Pauper Press, 2003.

Robert. *Cocktails, How to Mix Them*. London: H. Jenkins, 1922.

Rudin, Max. "There Is Something about a Martini," *American Heritage*, July–August 1997.

Saucier, Ted. *Bottom's Up*. 1951.

Schumann, Charles. *American Bar*. New York: Abbeville Press Publishers, 1991.

—. *The Tropical Bar Book—Drinks and Stories*. New York, Stewart, Tabori and Chang. 1986.

Sinclair, Andrew. *Prohibition: The Era of Excess*. Boston: Little, Brown, 1962.

Stewart, Amy. *The Drunken Botanist: The Plants That Create the World's Great Drinks*. Chapel Hill, N.C.: Algonquin Books of Chapel Hill, 2013.

Sullivan, Jack. *Mostly Whiskey—Bottles. Jugs & Whathaveyou*. Alexandria, Virginia, 2006.

Sundin, Knut W. *Two Hundred Selected Drinks*. Göteberg: Ragnar Orstadius, Boktryckeri, 1930. The "name" bartender for the Swedish-American Lines Prohibition "booze cruises."

Thomas, Jerry. *The Bar-Tender's Guide*. 1862.

Thompson, Neal. *Driving with the Devil: Southern Moonshine, Detroit Wheels, and the Birth of Nascar*. New York: Three Rivers Press, 2006.

Towne, Charles Hanson. *The Rise And Fall of Prohibition: the Human Side of What the Eighteenth Amendment And the Volstead Act Have Done to the United States*. New York: The Macmillan Company, 1923.

Umberger, Daryl. "The Martini." *St. James Encyclopedia of Popular Culture.* Ed. Thomas Riggs. 2nd ed. Vol. 3. Detroit: St. James Press, 2013. 472–73.

Van de Water, Frederic F. *The Real McCoy: The True Story of Captain Bill Mc-Coy of the Tomoka, the Founder of Rum Row and King of the Rum Runners.* Through a momumental stroke of good luck, I was able to obtain a copy of this book on eBay for a very reasonable price, considering the fact that it is inscribed on the title page by the subject Bill McCoy: "HEAD WINDS NEVER LAST FOREVER—AND OH BOY—HOW FAST WE SAIL WHEN THEY TURN FAIR—GOOD LUCK BILL MCCOY PALM BEACH FLORIDA MAY, ONE 1938."

Walker, Eric Sherbrooke. *The Confessions of a Rum-runner.* New York: I. Washburn, 1928.

Walker, Stanley. *The Night Club Era.* New York: Frederick A. Stokes, 1933

Wondrich, David. *Imbibe! From Absinthe Cocktail to Whiskey Smash, a Salute in Stories and Drinks Too.* New York: Perigee Trade, 2007.

WEBPAGES OF NOTE

"Bottles. Booze and Back Stories—A Blog About More Things Than You Can Shake a Stick At" Maintained by my old friend Jack Sullivan this blog is a trove of whiskey lore; bottlesboozeandbackstories.blogspot.com/.

The Cold Glass is a very useful and well-written cocktail blog written by a man named Doug Ford; cold-glass.com/.

NOTES

PREFACE

1. "Psst: the speakeasy returns: the prohibition era hideaway finds a new—secret—home." *Restaurant Business*, Apr. 2009: 20. "The modern speakeasy: a taboo's irresistible appeal." *Art Culinaire*, Spring 2010: 80.

2. Felicity Cloake, "The Modern Speakeasy: Felicity Cloake Celebrates a New and Sophisticated Golden Age of the Cocktail," *New Statesman (1996)*, September 19, 2011.

3. "Detroit dig uncovers hidden speakeasy." *Michigan History Magazine*, 98.1 (2014): 9; "Mystery whiskey bottle 'Belle of Dayton' deepens tale of downtown Dayton's secret speakeasy, pawn shop workers say." *Dayton Daily News* (Ohio), February 9, 2013.

CHAPTER 1: INTRODUCING "THE MAN IN THE GREEN HAT"

1. The act was named for Texas Senator Morris Sheppard on whose farm an illegal 130-gallon still was discovered during Prohibition. The fact that the farm was in Jollyville, Texas gave some the idea that the story was apocryphal, but it was true.

2. "When and How Prohibition Came to Washington," *The Washington Herald* December 7, 1931. In 1931, when the article appeared, there were more than two thousand illegal operations in the city.

3. George L. Cassiday, "Cassiday, Capitol Bootlegger, Got First Rum Order from Dry." *Washington Post*, October 25, 1930, p. 1. Cassiday seems to have gotten along as well with those who voted "Dry" as with those on the "Wet" side.

4. *Literary Digest*, "'The Man in the Green Hat' Uncovers," November 22, 1930; p. 10.

5. Edward T. Folliard, "White House Hedge Hid Bootleg Gin." *Washington Post*,

December 6, 1953, p. B-1. The fact that Folliard could talk about his "favorite bootlegger" in print underscored the degree to which the press was wet.

6. Ibid., 1.
7. Interview with Frederick Drum Hunt by Sarah Booth Conroy, *Washington Post*, October 4, 1993, p. B-3. "Prohibition? Bottoms Up!"
8. "Old-Timers Dwell on Shoomaker's Hey-Day Here," *Washington Daily News*, December 5, 1933.
9. Frederick Tilp, *This Was Potomac River* (1978), 290.
10. R. L Hartt, "Prohibition as It Is," *World's Work*, XLIX (1925), 511–12, quoted in Preston William Slosson, *The Great Crusade and After, 1914–1928*, vol. 12 (New York: Macmillan Company, 1930), 115.

CHAPTER 2: UNINTENDED CONSEQUENCES

1. Marni Davis, *Jews and Booze: Becoming American in the Age of Prohibition* (New York: New York University Press, 2012), 147.
2. Frederic F. Van de Water, *The Real McCoy* (New York: Doubleday, Doran & Company, 1931).
3. Herbert Asbury, *The Great Illusion: An Informal History of Prohibition* (Garden City, NY: Doubleday, 1950), 247.

CHAPTER 3: GOTHAM

1. Al Hirschfeld, *The Speakeasies of 1932* (Milwaukee, WI: Glenn Young Books, 2003), 9.
2. Preston William Slosson, *The Great Crusade and After, 1914–1928*, vol. 12 (New York: Macmillan Company, 1930).
3. "Oases Flourish Despite Gloom Along Rum Row," *New York Herald-Tribune*, May 14, 1925; p. 1.
4. Slosson, *The Great Crusade and After*, 123.
5. Irving Fisher, *Prohibition at Its Worst* (New York: Macmillan, 1926), 101.
6. William E. Masterson, *Jurisdiction in Marginal Seas: With Special Reference to Smuggling* (New York: Macmillan, 1929), 358.
7. Cab Calloway and Bryant Rollins, *Of Minnie the Moocher and Me*, ed. John Shearer (New York: Thomas Y. Crowell Company, 1976), 11.
8. Saul Pett, "Speakeasy Bouncer Remembers Fun and Frolic of the Twenties." *Milwaukee Journal*, July 18, 1958; p. 12.

CHAPTER 4: THE RISE OF THE COCKTAIL CULTURE

1. H. L. Mencken, *The American Language: An Inquiry into the Development of English in the United States*, 2nd rev. ed. (New York: Alfred A. Knopf, 1921), 99.

2. Max Rudin, "There Is Something about a Martini," *American Heritage*, July–August 1997.

3. Ibid.

4. *The Armchair James Beard*, p. 196.

5. William Johnson, "Some Inside Stuff about New York," *The Sunday Star*, December 24, 1922; p. 16. Also *Evening Star*, December 27, 1922; p. 1.

6. George Ade, *The Old Time Saloon* (New York: Ray Long and Richard R. Smith, 1931), 51.

7. Andrew Sinclair, *Prohibition: The Era of Excess* (Boston: Little, Brown, 1962), 239.

8. Sir Arthur Conan Doyle, "Our American Adventure," *The Evening Star*, October 19, 1922, p. 6.

9. Sinclair Lewis, *Babbitt*, 161.

10. Tom Pettey, "Dry Law Solves Christmas Gift Problem in N.Y.," *Chicago Tribune*, December 17, 1928; p. 19.

11. Tori Avey of the History Kitchen made this assertion May 14, 2013.

12. George Jean Nathan and H. L. Mencken, *The American Mercury*, September 1924; pp. 57–63.

13. Sinclair (Boston, 1962), 233.

14. "Hergesesheimer Off, Flees 'Bathtub gin,'" *New York Times*, September 1, 1932; p. 23.

15. Cab Calloway and Bryant Rollins, *Of Minnie the Moocher and Me*, ed. John Shearer (New York: Thomas Y. Crowell Company, 1976), 10.

16. "Exiled Bartenders Ready to Return When Wanted Here," *Atlanta Constitution*, June 5, 1926; p. 10.

CHAPTER 5: THE COCKTAIL AS ART AND ENTERTAINMENT

1. "Cocktail Hour's Origin Disputed, But All of the Authorities Agree That It's Old American Custom," *New York Herald-Tribune*, June 19, 1934; p. A3.

2. Sinclair Lewis, *The Man Who Knew Coolidge* (New York: Harcourt Brace and Company, 1928), 20-1. 60.

3. John C. Burnham, ed., *Bad Habits: Drinking, Smoking, Taking Drugs, Gambling, Sexual Misbehavior and Swearing in American History* (American Social Experience) (New York: New York University Press, 1994), 37.

4. Marion Elizabeth Rodgers, *Mencken: The American Iconoclast* (New York: Oxford University Press, 2005), 212.

5. Roy A. Haynes, *Prohibition inside Out* (Garden City, NY: Doubleday, Page, 1923), 307.

6. Regan, *The Joy of Mixology* (New York: Clarkson Potter, 2003), 28.

CHAPTER 7: THE ARCHAEOLOGY OF THE COCKTAIL

1. H. L. Mencken, *The American Language: An Inquiry into the Development of English in the United States*, 2nd Rev. ed. (New York: Alfred A. Knopf, 1921), 99. The manuals Mencken mentioned by name are: *The Hoffman House Bartender's Guide*, by Charles Mahoney, 4th ed. (New York, 1916); in *The Barkeeper's Manual*, by Raymond E. Sullivan, 4th ed. (Baltimore, n.d.); and in *Wehman Brothers' Bartenders' Guide* (New York, 1912).

2. H. L. Mencken, "Books about Boozing," *The American Mercury*, October 1930; pp. 252–54.

3. Neil A. Grauer, "The Speakeasies I Remember: In a Last Conversation Before His Death at 99 This January, the Artist Recalled the Places He Visited, Drew, and Wrote About During Prohibition in New York City. You Can Still Lift a Glass at a Couple of Them. (Al Hirschfeld)," *American Heritage*, June–July 2003.

CHAPTER 9: DUFFY'S ASTERISKS

1. Salvatore Calabrese, *Classic Cocktails* (New York: Main Street, 2006), 122.

2. William Grimes, *Straight Up or On the Rocks: A Cultural History of American Drink* (New York: Simon & Schuster, 1993), 103.

3. "Police Storm Deluxe Club, Seize Liquor," *Washington Post*, November 4, 1933.

CHAPTER 10: THE FORMULARY—AKA "LIBERTY'S LIBATIONS"

1. William Guyer, *The Merry Mixer or Cocktails and Their Ilk: a Booklet On Mixtures and Mulches, Fizzes and Whizzes* (New York: Jos. S. Finch & Co., 1933), 18.

2. www.esquire.com/drinks/between-the-sheets-drink-recipe.

3. "How to Throw a Sure-Fire Party," *Washington Post*, August 3, 1930; p. SM6.

4. "Holiday Hangover," *Daily Herald* (Arlington Heights, IL), January 2, 2009.

5. Burns, Eric, *The Spirits of America: A Social History of Alcohol* (Philadelphia: Temple University Press, 2004), 198–99.

6. Grosset & Dunlap, *Esquire's Handbook for Hosts* (New York: Funk & Wagnalls Company, 1949), 180.

7. Tallulah Bankhead, *Tallulah: My Autobiography* (New York: Harper, 1952), 95.

8. Beard, James, "Bloody Mary less Worcestershire? Bloody awful!" *Washington Star*, September 19, 1979.

9. Al Hirschfeld, Al, *The Speakeasies of 1932* (Milwaukee, WI: Glenn Young Books, 2003), 54.

10. Fougner, G. Selmer, *Along the Wine Trail Vol V* (The Sun Printing and Publishing Association, 1937), 98.

11. Albert Stevens Crockett, *Old Waldorf Bar Days*, 1st ed. (New York: Aventine Press, 1931), 80–81.

12. "Bill W., 75, Dies; Cofounder Of Alcoholics Anonymous," *New York Times*, January 27, 1971.

13. "The Navy Doctor & The Daiquiri," *The Grog: A Journal of Navy Medical History and Culture*, Spring 2011: 23.

14. Sterling North, *So Red the Nose, Or, Breath in the Afternoon* (New York: Farrar & Rinehart, 1935), 8.

15. Baker, Charles H. Jr., *The Gentleman's Companion*, Volume II (New York: Crown Publishers, 1946), 31.

16. Grosset & Dunlap, *Esquire's Handbook for Hosts*, 116.

17. Neil A. Grauer, "The Speakeasies I Remember: In a Last Conversation before His Death at 99 This January, the Artist Recalled the Places He Visited, Drew, and Wrote about during Prohibition in New York City. You Can Still Lift a Glass at a Couple of Them."

18. Norman H. Clark, *Deliver Us from Evil: An Interpretation of American Prohibition*, The Norton Essays in American History (New York: Norton, 1976), 213.

19. Richard Hughes, *A High Wind in Jamaica* (1929), 77.

20. H. L. Mencken, *The American Language: An Inquiry into the Development of English in the United States*, 2nd Rev. ed. (New York: Alfred A. Knopf, 1921), 99.

21. Peter Tamony, "Martini Cocktail," *Western Folklore*, 26, no. 2. April 1, 1967.

22. Max Rudin, "There Is Something about a Martini," *American Heritage*, July–August 1997.

23. Max Rudin, "There Is Something About a Martini. (Cover Story)," *American Heritage* 48, no. 4 (July 1997); 32.

24. Barnaby Conrad, *The Martini: An Illustrated History of an American Classic* (San Francisco: Chronicle Books, 1995), 67–68.

25. "Nixon in Rebozoland," *Saturday Review*, March 8, 1969; 109.

26. From About.Com, "Hollywood Cocktails."

27. Brian Carpenter, "The South's Thirsty Muse," *Southern Cultures*, 6, no. 1, 2000.

28. "Book by Mrs. Doan Gives 83 Ginless Punch Recipes," *Washington Post*, September 10, 1930; 1.

29. Michael A. Lerner, *Dry Manhattan: Prohibition in New York City* (Cambridge, MA: Harvard University Press, 2007).

30. Meigs O. Frost, "Creole Kitchens Monarchs Wait," *Evening Star* (published as *The Sunday Star*), April 18, 1937; 62.

31. Quoting directly from *The Boston Herald* of January 16, 1924. "Delcevare King of Quincy last night announced that 'scofflaw' is the winning word in the contest for the $200 he offered for a word, to characterize the 'lawless drinker' of illegally made or illegally obtained liquor. 'Scofflaw' was chosen from more than 25,000 words, submitted from all the states and from several foreign countries. The word was sent by two contestants, so the prize will be equally divided between Henry Irving Dale and Miss Kate L. Butler."

32. Roy A. Haynes, *Prohibition Inside Out.* (Garden City, NY: Doubleday, 1923), 73.

33. Fletcher Dobyns. *The Amazing Story of Repeal; an exposé of the power of propaganda* (Chicago: Willett, Clark & Company, 1940), 185.

34. *Prohibition at Its Worst* (New York: Macmillan, 1926), 72.

GLOSSARY OF VOLSTEAD ENGLISH

1. *Minnesota Gen. Statutes Suppl.* (1888), 248.

2. Herbert Asbury, *The Great Illusion: An Informal History of Prohibition* (Garden City, NY: Doubleday, 1950), 24.

3. Federal Writers' Project, *Kentucky: A Guide to the Bluegrass State* (New York: Harcourt, Brace, 1939), 225.

4. Slosson, *The Great Crusade and After*, 117.

5. Mencken, *The American Language*, 99.

6. Roy A. Haynes, *Prohibition inside Out* (Garden City, NY: Doubleday, 1923).

7. Stanley Walker, *The Night Club Era* (New York: Frederick A. Stokes, 1933), 69.

8. Walker, 9.

9. *New York Herald Tribune*, March 1, 1924; 1.

10. *Online Encyclopedia of Washington State History*: www.historylink.org/This_week/index.cfm.

11. Thomas B. Allen, *Declassified: 50 Top-Secret Documents That Changed History* (Washington, D.C.: National Geographic, 2008), 273 Olmstead v. United States, 277 U.S. 438 (1928).

INDEX

ABOUT THE AUTHOR

PAUL DICKSON is the author of more than sixty-five books and hundreds articles on the American language, baseball, and twentieth-century history. His previous book for Melville House was *Drunk: The Drinker's Dictionary*, which was recognized by the *Guinness Book of World Records* as the largest-ever collection of synonyms. He lives in Maryland, with his wife, Nancy.